1960s

American Cars of the
1960s

By the Auto Editors of
Consumer Guide®

Publications International, Ltd.

Louis Weber, CEO
Publications International, Ltd.
7373 North Cicero Avenue
Lincolnwood, Illinois 60712

Manufactured in China.

8 7 6 5 4 3 2 1

ISBN-13: 978-1-4508-0641-1
ISBN-10: 1-4508-0641-4

Library of Congress Control Number: 2004113593

The images in this book were reproduced from original
manufacturer brochures, advertisements, and factory photos.
We thank the various manufacturers for the use of these images
and for the creativity shown by the talented artists of the day.

A special thanks to the photgraphers whose images were used in this book:

Sam Griffith; Scott Hutchinson; Bud Juneau; Dan Lyons; Vince Manocchi;
Doug Mitchel; Mike Mueller; Richard Spiegelman; David Talbot;
David Temple; Bob Tenney; Nicky Wright.

TABLE OF CONTENTS

FOREWORD

These pages celebrate an American industry and an American art form. They trace 1960s automotive styling, as the gaudy look typical of 1950s Detroit gave way to more tasteful design. Car buyers changed too, and that led to new sizes and types of cars, particularly sporty performance models. Here, also, is a transformation in how Detroit portrayed and promoted its cars. Brochures and ads heavy on illustrations in the early '60s evolved into more realistic photo-based pieces, more serious statements for increasingly serious times.

9

1960 BUICK

Like other General Motors cars of 1960, Buicks were toned-down versions of the all-new 1959 models, though Buick's basic "delta wing" design was still pretty wild. The facelift did revive Buick's trademark: front-fender "venti-ports." Top-line Electras and Electra 225s had four of the decorative accents, vs. three for midrange Invictas and entry-level LeSabres. The '60s also wore a prominent new "tri-shield" Buick logo.

10

Though two- and four-door hardtops remained Buick's bread-and-butter for 1960, the lineup included a lone two-door sedan in LeSabre trim, three convertibles, and a LeSabre Estate Wagon. A nine-passenger wagon with a rear-facing third-row seat was a new 1960 alternative to the six-seat model.

1961

The 1961 Buicks were fully redesigned with much cleaner styling. The costlier the model, the more front-fender "portholes."

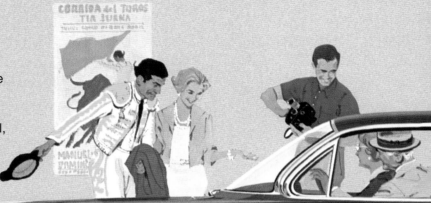

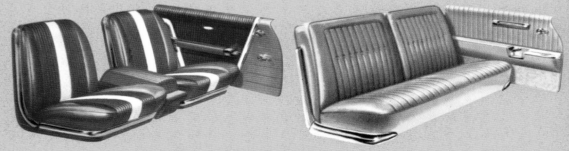

The '61 Buicks not only looked leaner but actually weighed a bit less than the 1960 models. Interior trim was keyed to series: upscale on entry-level LeSabres (hardtop coupe above), opulent on Electra 225s (hardtop sedan below).

13

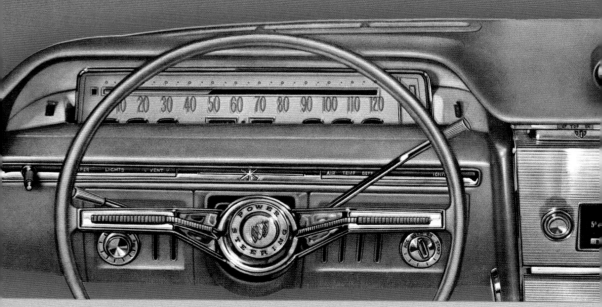

Reflecting the growing popularity of compact cars was Buick's new 1961 Special (below, far right). It bowed as a sedan and wagon with a lively little 215-cubic-inch V-8 as standard. Big Buicks sported a jazzy new dashboard with a speedometer that reflected onto a tilt-adjustable mirror.

14

15

1962

Full-size Buicks got a more-conservative look for 1962, but among them was a Wildcat, a new hardtop coupe (below). It had bucket seats, vinyl-covered roof, and other unique touches. It was quite the elegant hot rod with a standard 325-horsepower V-8. Adding appeal to Buick's compact Special line were new convertible and coupe models, which were available in sporty Skylark trim with bucket seats. For Buick and all Detroit, "think young" was the order of the day.

Though respected for its brawny V-8s, Buick introduced a V-6 as standard power for its 1962 Special compacts (top row). It was the first such engine in U.S. production, and proved quite popular.

'63

Long regarded as a modern design classic, Buick's all-new 1963 Riviera (right) was General Motors' first direct challenger to the popular Ford Thunderbird in the growing "personal-luxury" market. Like most full-size Buicks, it came with a 325-horsepower 401 V-8, but a new 425 V-8 with 340 horses was an exclusive Riviera option. Meantime, big Buicks adopted crisper new lines, and the sporty Wildcat added hardtop sedan (above) and convertible models.

'64 "When better automobiles are built,

Big-Buick styling was further refined for 1964. Wildcats (like the yellow convertible shown) were easily spotted by specific "ventiports" placed low on the front fenders. Standard rear fender skirts were a new marker for flagship Electra 225s (above right). Entry-level LeSabres (far right) were also restrained. This year's dashboards looked like something from a NASA space capsule, but a tilt-up steering wheel was a useful new option, and interior trim choices were as varied as ever.

RIVIERA

Buick will build them."

ELECTRA 225

LeSABRE/WILDCAT

WILDCAT

RIVIERA

'65

Riviera looked better than ever for 1965, with headlights newly concealed behind "clamshell" doors flanking the grille. Many luxury-car buyers now craved big power and sporty road manners, and they found much to like in Riviera's new Gran Sport package. Included were a 425 "Wildcat" V-8 with a stout 360 horsepower, plus a firmer suspension and fat tires on styled steel wheels for tauter, more-precise handling.

Buick's newly enlarged compacts returned for 1965 with a popular midsize package offering a V-6 and three optional V-8s. With "muscle car mania" sweeping the land, many buyers opted for the suave new Skylark Gran Sport hardtop or convertible with a potent 325-horsepower 400 V-8, plus uprated suspension, bucket seats, and other "hot car" features.

GM restyled all its full-size cars for 1965.
Buicks fared well, gaining curvier lines without losing the brand's conservative, upscale
elegance. Body-trim variations made it easy
to distinguish, say, a LeSabre (above) from
sporty Wildcats (right and below).

Introducing the tuned car. 1966 Buick.

*What makes a car a car is styling, performance, ride and handling. Only when they're all tuned together is the car a Buick.
Like this 1966 Electra 225.*

You know how well your car's engine runs after a tuneup? Buick tuning has the same effect on the whole car. Not just the engine. The whole Buick. Everything blends with everything else. Styling. Performance. Ride. Handling. All tuned to work together in harmony. That's what the tuned car is. A Buick.

Can the tuned car really do anything for you that ordinary cars can't?

Stop, look and listen. And see.

What you can learn from a look. The beauty of a '66 Buick's beauty is that it goes beyond looks. Because we style the tuned car to look like a million dollars—and then build it as if looks didn't count.

So things *fit* on a Buick. The doors. The hood. Carpeting. You can see attention to detail wherever you look. (The reason we're so attentive is that Buick owners have a long history of being attentive themselves. They're used to the best, and we aim to please.)

And things *blend*, too. You don't get the feeling that the rear deck doesn't belong with the grille, or that the interior doesn't really quite fit in. That's tuned styling.

What a listen can tell you. Buick thinks building a quiet car is more than a matter of insulation. In fact, we build our cars as if insulation never existed. We winnow out sound before it starts.

And when we have the car as silent as we can make it, we apply insulation. Just the right amount, just where it'll do the most good.

And so when you go driving, you don't hear a lot of little intrusions. But you do feel the road. We think road feel is important, in the tuned car. (Our engineers spend vast amounts of time out on the road, testing and checking and re-testing. It's said that our chief engineer won't approve a design until we build it and he or his staff can test it.)

A drive can do more. Now that you've been introduced to the tuned car, you should meet it personally. The Electra 225 in our picture is perhaps the ultimate Buick. (It answers the question, "What do you move up to when you've been used to a Buick?") Among its standard features are power steering and brakes, Super Turbine automatic transmission and virtually everything you can think of to make driving pure pleasure.

Driving the tuned car will teach you more than you might suspect.

For one thing, you'll find out why Buick owners are so loyal. And so many.

Wouldn't you really rather have a Buick?

1966

Full-size Buicks got no drastic change for 1966. Still, engineering tweaks improved quietness and ride comfort a bit, so that year's new "tuned car" ad slogan wasn't all hype. On the other hand, the brand's umbrella line—"Wouldn't you really have a Buick?"—had become a national catchphrase. Even some comedians and politicans used variations on the theme. Happily for Buick, it helped to keep sales healthy.

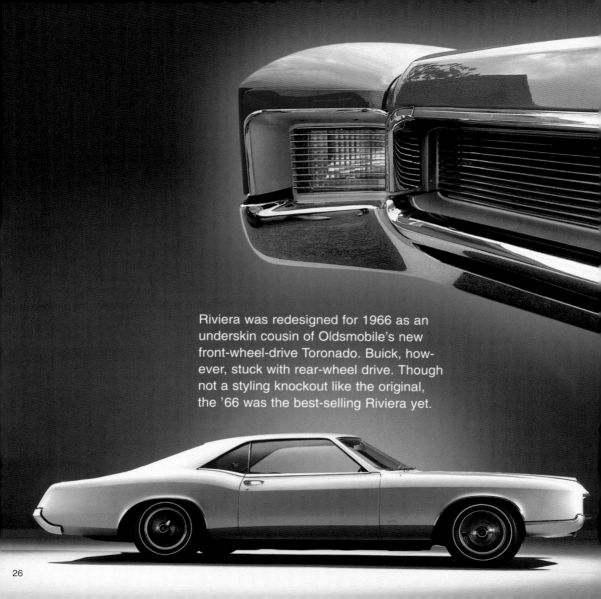

Riviera was redesigned for 1966 as an underskin cousin of Oldsmobile's new front-wheel-drive Toronado. Buick, however, stuck with rear-wheel drive. Though not a styling knockout like the original, the '66 was the best-selling Riviera yet.

Buick's new GS-340. The minipriced GS-400.

Our now-famous GS-400 (which you see lurking in the background) doesn't come for peanuts. It's a great car—but just a little rich for some people. So we set to work and designed the Buick GS-340. It has a smaller engine (but it weighs a lot less). Its interior isn't quite as sumptuous (but it's clean and simple and tasteful). It has its own exterior paint: a broad rally stripe, and contrasting hood scoops. And its own orna- mentation and the full complement of GM safety features. We ended up with a car that does indeed cost less than the GS-400. But one with its own brand of excitement. Give one a drive soon. It's maxidriving.

"When better automobiles are built, Buick will build them." Still true.

'67

Realizing that its potent 340-horsepower GS-400 muscle cars were "just a little rich for some people," Buick added a GS-340 hardtop for 1967. Named for its 340 cubic-inch V-8, it had "only" 260 horses, but was much like the 400 hardtop otherwise—and cost $200 less. Hood scoops and body stripes were among the shared features.

27

Full-size Buicks had a new look for 1967, highlighted by flowing "sweepspear" bodyside lines, a nod to 1950s Buick styling. Ads like this revived Buick's famous "better automobiles" slogan.

The best of everything Buick. Electra 225.

This is the Buick Buick owners look up to. And that's saying something. This sophisticated blend of styling, performance, ride and handling takes on new luster for 1967. New security, too, with all of the new GM safety features. And standard equipment that includes power brakes, power steering, and a 430-cu. in. V-8. Electra 225 gives new meaning to our famous theme: When better automobiles are built, Buick will build them.

Electra 225

Electra 225 Custom Sport Coupe

Electra 225 Sport Coupe

Electra 225 Limited 4-dr. Hardtop (Trim Option)

Electra 225 Custom 4-dr. Hardtop

Electra 225 Custom 4-dr. Sedan

Electra 225 4-dr. Sedan

Electra 225 Custom Convertible

'68

Buick often aimed to steal luxury-car thunder from sister division Cadillac. Its 1968 Electra 225s were but one example. Besides "base" and fancier Custom interiors, the flagship line offered a new Limited trim option with premium cloth or leather upholstery to rival anything Cadillac used. Available for four-door models, the Limited package also included a vinyl roof covering, special badges—and that extra dollop of prestige.

29

Midsize Buicks gained "sweepspear" styling with a 1968 redesign that put two-door models on a shorter chassis than the four-doors. The makeover introduced a novel "vista dome" roof for the top-line Sportwagon (left), which was available with pseudo-wood trim.

Buick Sportwagon comes with 2 or 3 seats, a 220-hp V-8 engine and a carpeted passenger area. Custom padded cushions are standard. So is a full line of GM safety equipment which includes a four way hazard warning flasher and energy absorbing steering column.

"It looks more like a luxury car than a station wagon!"

"Any given weekend, we carry boats, sails, masts, five or six children, picnic baskets, saddles, bridles, tack trunks, blankets— we even pack a nine-foot dinghy in the back of our Buick Sportwagon."

Mrs. Graham Brown, Mother of five.

Wouldn't you really rather have a Buick?

"The children stretch out in the back, gaze up at the stars through the sun roof and they're off to sleep in no time."

GS 350

1968

Though less fiery than some other muscle cars, the new-look 1968 GS-400 (right) and GS-350 combined plentiful power with Buick's typical upscale appointments.

'68 Buick. Now we're talking your language.

We changed the Skylark from front to rear, we gave it a whole new look, simply because we believe you want a car like this. In other words, we're talking your language.

All Buicks have the full line of General Motors safety features as standard equipment. [...] ole, seat back latches and padded [...] orner posts.

We thought you'd like to have a little easier time parking. So we shortened the wheelbase of the two-door Skylark down to 112 inches. Wouldn't you really rather have a Buick?

1969

Riviera looked more imposing for 1969 via a massive "loop-style" bumper grille. The outboard ends housed large parking/turn-signal lamps. Headlights remained out of sight except at night, when they powered down from the top of the grille. A standard 430 V-8 delivered 360 horsepower.

New bodies with new variation on familiar styling themes marked Buick's full-size cars for 1969. As on the latest Riviera, front-door vent windows were eliminated in favor of a more-effective—and quieter—flow-through interior ventilation system.

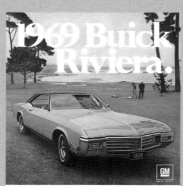

1969 Buick Riviera.

No wonder Buick owners keep selling Buicks for us.

The look is new, personal and impressive.

But the look isn't all that's impressive. The 1969 Riviera has Buick's revolutionary new suspension system. It's a major suspension refinement that affords straight sure tracking.

And there's an upper level ventilating system on the new Riviera. It adds an impressive amount of comfort and eliminates side vent windows and wind noise and uncomfortable drafts that go with them.

Standard equipment includes a 430 cubic inch V8, automatic transmission, power steering, power brakes, concealed headlamps and more. Much more.

Very impressive.

Safety and anti-theft features. The 1969 Riviera has an impressive list, including the energy absorbing steering column and a new ignition, steering and a new ignition, steering you lock your ignition, steering column and transmission controls when you turn off the key.

You're impressed? You have every right to be.

Want to hear more? Then see your Buick dealer and the 1969 Buick Riviera. Make your favorable impression a complete one.

Wouldn't you really rather have a Buick?

Electra 225

No wonder Buick owners keep selling Buicks for us.

Wouldn't you really rather have a Buick?

33

1960

Cadillac's 1959 styling was the height of Fifties flamboyance. Designers dialed back for the new decade, making the 1960 models more restrained, with lower tailfins and less gaudy grilles immediately evident. Convertibles, as always, were the glamour leaders, comprising a mainstream Series 62 model (above) and the limited-edition Eldorado Biarritz (right). Both used 390-cubic-inch V-8s like other models, but the Eldo offered 345 horses vs. 325.

1961

Cadillac was all-new for 1961, shedding a few inches and pounds while gaining a crisp, chiseled look. Highlighting the new design were lower-body "skeg fins" and arched windshield posts—no more Fifties-faddish "doglegs" to bang knees. Cadillac still offered more models by far than rivals Lincoln and Imperial, one reason General Motors' flagship remained America's luxury sales leader. All '61 Cadillacs used the division's 325-horse-power 390 V-8.

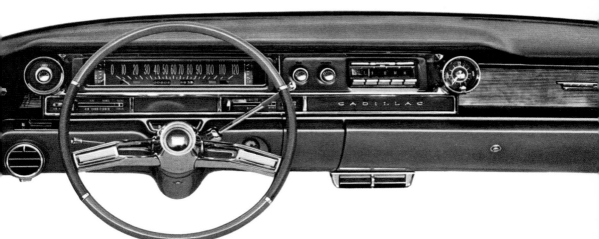

Typical of the time, Cadillac's 1961 instrument panel had few gauges and plenty of dazzling chrome—plus an extra-wide glovebox door. Interiors were as opulent as ever. Bucket-type seats were available for the toney Eldorado Biarritz convertible (left). Other models featured posh cloth-covered bench seats front and rear with wide pulldown center armrests.

1962

Cadillac's 1962 styling was a more-conservative take on the new '61 look. Again topping the 13-model lineup was the regal Fleetwood Seventy-Five, offered as a nine-passenger sedan and as the limousine pictured at right. It was 20 feet long. Price was equally grand at around $10,000. Most were built to special order. Cadillac number 2.5 million, a mainstream Series 62 hardtop coupe (as shown at lower right) rolled off the line in 1962.

'63 Another redesign helped Cadillac to a new sales record of more than 163,000 for 1963. The division also reworked its V-8 engine for the first time in 14 years, making it lighter, more fuel efficient, smoother, and more reliable. Horsepower was still 325, but Cadillacs shed a few pounds, so performance improved, with 0-60 mph down to only about 10 seconds. No wonder sales were so good!

Cadillac
1964

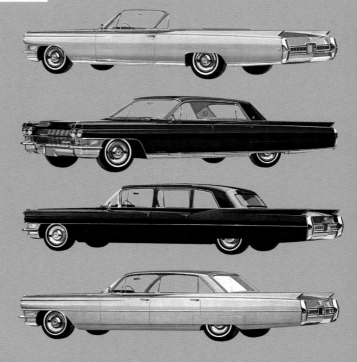

Cadillac's once-soaring tailfins were down to modest fendertop blades for 1964—which made the cars look even longer and lower. A new grille with a body-color divider bar enhanced visual width, but exterior dimensions were basically the same as for '63. Besides this effective facelift, Cadillac offered a larger 429 V-8 for '64. It generated a whopping 340 horsepower. Also new was an available heating/air-conditioning system that automatically maintained a set temperature. Ever the luxury innovator, Cadillac remained America's luxury favorite and set another sales record this year.

43

1965

Cadillac sales zoomed to nearly 200,000 for banner 1965. Yet another redesign produced the trimmest Caddys in many a year, highlighted by stacked headlamps and gently curved side windows.

1965

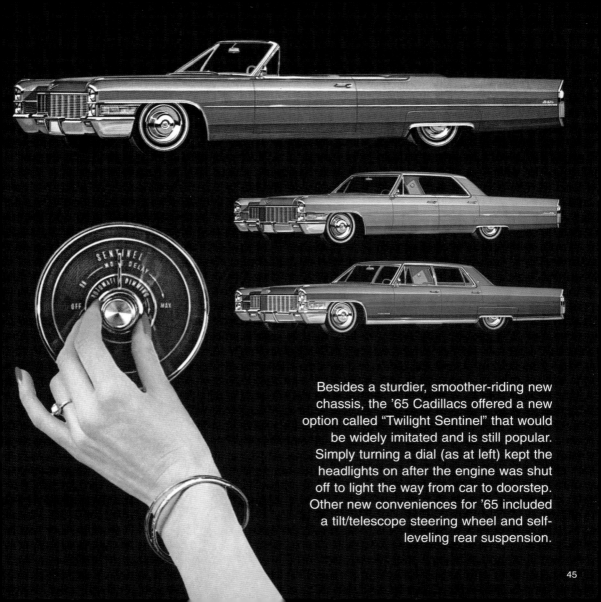

Besides a sturdier, smoother-riding new chassis, the '65 Cadillacs offered a new option called "Twilight Sentinel" that would be widely imitated and is still popular. Simply turning a dial (as at left) kept the headlights on after the engine was shut off to light the way from car to doorstep. Other new conveniences for '65 included a tilt/telescope steering wheel and self-leveling rear suspension.

1966

The '66 Cadillacs reprised the successful '65 formula, albeit with minor styling tweaks and two new options: variable-ratio power steering, for sportier handling, and heated front seats— another industry first. Also new was a Fleetwood Brougham sedan with vinyl roof covering and extra-posh interior (far right). Despite little-changed looks, model-year sales broke 200,000 for the first time.

SOME OF OUR BEST FRIENDS ARE CHAUFFEURS. And there are a number of reasons why: the car's exceptional comfort, its great interior luxury, its new smoothness and quietness of operation, the marvelous ease provided by Cadillac's new steering and handling, and, of course, the car's impressive new stature and beauty. No wonder that wherever you find Cadillac chauffeurs—professional or amateur—you find a solid body of praise for the 1966 Cadillac, the world's most highly regarded luxury car. Drive it soon at your authorized dealer's. You'll discover why Cadillac makes friends so easily. *New elegance, new excellence, new excitement!*

1967

Eldorado was boldly transformed for 1967, from rear-wheel-drive convertible to an elegant front-wheel-drive "personal" coupe. Though based on Oldsmobile's year-old Toronado, it offered a smoother, quieter ride with the same assured handling. Of course, it used Cadillac's own 340-horsepower 429 V-8. Hidden headlamps announced sporty, yet dignified, styling. The interior was spacious. Many regard this design as one of Cadillac's best.

ELDORADO
World's finest personal car

50

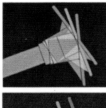

Though overshadowed by the reborn Eldorado, Cadillac's mainstream '67s offered fresh styling, a new-look dashboard, and extra standard features like tilt/telescope steering wheel (left) and cruise control. Fleetwood sedans also added rear self-leveling (illustrated above). The DeVille convertible was now Cadillac's only ragtop. As ever, the Sedan deVille and Coupe deVille hardtops were the line's most popular models.

1968

Elegance in action!

Air-pollution laws took effect for 1968, and Cadillac was ready with a new 472 V-8. It ran cleaner than the 429 it replaced, and delivered 35 more horsepower, a rousing 375 in all. Sales were down a bit for the model year, but still quite healthy.

The government also dictated side-marker lights and other new safety features for 1968. They were among the few visual changes for Eldorado (lower left) but senior Cadillacs also sported new grilles and, thanks to longer hoods, hidden windshield wipers.

Appropriate for America's luxury leader, advertising for the '68 Cadillacs posed various models in realistic, suitably upscale settings, reinforced by close-ups to highlight the lavish interiors. The popular Coupe deVille hardtop is the subject here. Broacde-type seat cloth looks dated now, but was *de rigueur* at the time.

55

Presenting Cadillac 1969

A masterpiece from the master craftsmen

Senior Cadillacs retained familar styling themes for 1969, but had all-new bodies that eliminated front vent windows. Contours became slightly blockier, and headlamps reverted to horizontal. Front head restraints, energy-absorbing steering column, and ignition-key warning buzzer were among new government-mandated standard features.

Cadillac still offered America's broadest luxury-car roster for 1969,
including a limousine-like Fleetwood Brougham sedan (above, left).
The hardtop Sedan deVille remained the most popular model in the
line. The '69 Eldorado (right) sported a fresh face with exposed headlamps, but Cadillac's modern classic was otherwise little-changed.

59

'60 CHEVROLET
NEAREST TO PERFECTION A LOW-PRICED CAR EVER CAME!

Perennial sales leader Chevrolet was in the second—and final—year of its "bat-wing" tail styling for its standard passenger cars. Critics—and buyers—approved. This magazine ad features the clean-looking Bel Air Sport Coupe hardtop (below) and its upscale Impala sibling.

1960

61

CORVAIR

Detroit's Big Three debuted compact cars for 1960. Chevy's Corvair was the most radical by far. Instead of a water-cooled engine in front, Corvair used a unique air-cooled "flat" six-cylinder placed at the rear—"where the engine belongs," said Chevy ads. That meant luggage stored in the nose, as in the popular Volkswagen Beetle, only Corvair had lots more space. It bowed in coupe and sedan models starting at just $1984.

MONZA

HAPPIEST DRIVING CAR IN ITS CLASS!

Chevrolet scored a surprise hit during 1960 with the Monza, a sporty Corvair coupe dressed up with bucket-type seats, floorshift, and upscale vinyl interior. Buyers loved its blend of American style and European road manners, and sales took off.

'61 CHEVROLET

Chevrolet's Corvette sports car got a jaunty "ducktail" rear end in a 1961 update that also included new performance options for weekend racers. Corvette set a new sales record for '61 at 10,939.

1961

Without greatly changing in size, Chevrolet's mainstay passenger models adopted graceful new styling for 1961. They looked lighter and more agile—which they were. Top-line Impalas (right) came with more bright trim than mid-priced Bel Airs (above), but all were neat and trim, with a fairly simple grille and artful "gull-wing" sculpturing at the rear. Chevy also offered station wagons with names like Nomad and Parkwood, plus a sturdy six-cylinder base engine and V-8s with up to 360 horsepower.

Chevy built 169,000 full-size wagons for '61, 32,000 more than runner-up Ford.

1962

Many car lovers rate the 1962 "standard" Chevys as one of the decade's best styling jobs. Impalas still sported triple tail-lamps, and the Sport Coupe (above) got a rear roofline with the look of a top-up convertible. Huge trunks with a deep center well were a big-Chevy plus. So was performance, especially in bucket-seat Impala SS models with a high-power V-8.

Impala's SS, or Super Sport, option continued for '62 as a $54 trim package for the convertible and hardtop coupe. Included was a passenger "grab bar" on the dashboard. Bucket seats cost $102.

The new-for-'62
compact Chevy II
matched Ford's
popular Falcon
with a simple,
orthodox design,
plus a sporty con-
vertible and hard-
top coupe that
Ford didn't offer.
Chevy's Corvair
(below) now sold
mostly to sports-
car lovers.

1963

Chevrolet's Corvette was brilliantly transformed inside and out with 1963's lighter, more-agile new Sting Ray. A true world-class sports car, it came as a convertible and as this stunning fastback coupe. The coupe's rear "split window" design turned out to be a one-year-only feature, but it helped qualify the '63 as an all-time Corvette classic. The new twin-cowl dashboard carried on the performance theme.

Chevrolet's 1963 lineup had something for most everyone, from compact Corvairs and Chevy IIs to big, "Jet Smooth" full-size cars like the posh, potent Impala SS hardtop. It was the same story all over Detroit, as car buyers were no longer satified with "one size fits all." Chevy kept satisfying them better than anyone else to remain atop the sales chart—"USA-1."

1964

Chevrolet again expanded its lineup with the 1964 Chevelle, a "midsize" car that reminded many of the "classic" mid-1950s Chevys. In price as well as size and power, Chevelle slotted between the compact Chevy II and full-size Chevrolets. Buyers took to it right away.

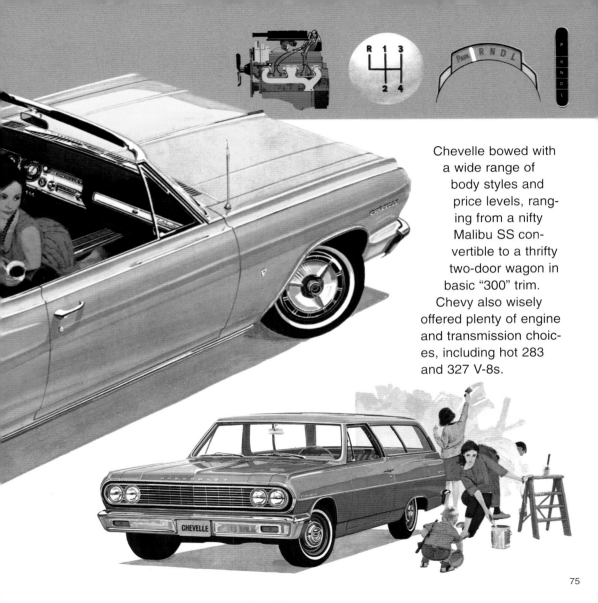

Chevelle bowed with a wide range of body styles and price levels, ranging from a nifty Malibu SS convertible to a thrifty two-door wagon in basic "300" trim. Chevy also wisely offered plenty of engine and transmission choices, including hot 283 and 327 V-8s.

CHEVELLE

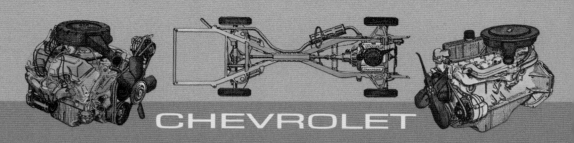

CHEVROLET

Full-size Chevys got a more-formal look for 1964, when the Impala SS hardtop coupe (below) and convertible became distinct models. Engine choices were as broad as ever, ranging from two time-proven sixes to no fewer than six V-8s, including a "real fine" 409 offering up to 425 horsepower.

Corvette

The Corvette Sting Ray coupe lost its "split-window" styling for 1964, but available horsepower hit a mighty 375. Four-wheel independent suspension aided control in corners and on straightaways.

1965

Chevy gave its Corvair and full-size cars a more-flowing look for 1965. This rather fanciful illustration shows a new Corvair four-door hardtop and a handsome Impala SS convertible whizzing above a Chevelle sedan and Chevy II Nova hardtop coupe, with a Corvette Sting Ray coupe at the far left. Chevy set a new record in what was a banner sales year for all of Detroit.

79

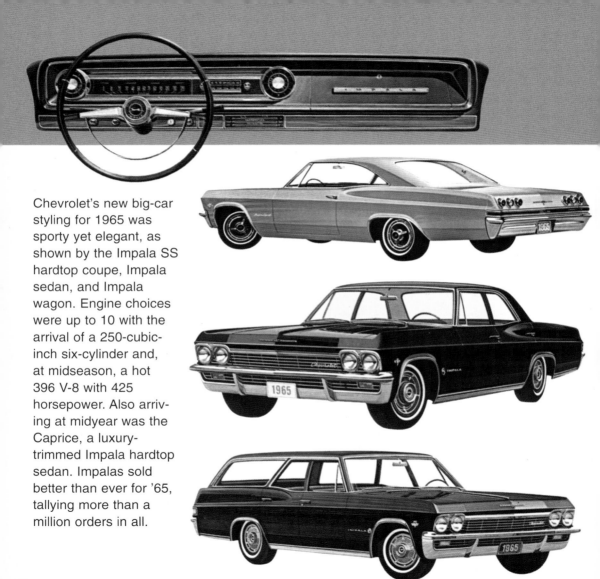

Chevrolet's new big-car styling for 1965 was sporty yet elegant, as shown by the Impala SS hardtop coupe, Impala sedan, and Impala wagon. Engine choices were up to 10 with the arrival of a 250-cubic-inch six-cylinder and, at midseason, a hot 396 V-8 with 425 horsepower. Also arriving at midyear was the Caprice, a luxury-trimmed Impala hardtop sedan. Impalas sold better than ever for '65, tallying more than a million orders in all.

Corvair was fully redesigned for 1965. Its handsome styling still looks good, and chassis revisions made handling both more predictable and even sportier. Coupes and sedans became pillarless hardtops models, led by the popular Monza four-door. The spunky turbocharged Corsa convertible was top of the line.

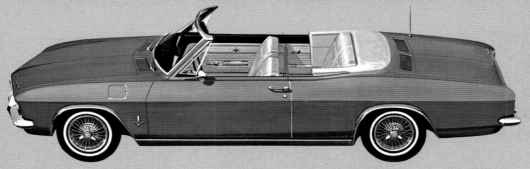

'66 CAPRICE

Chevrolet's eight-year push toward the luxury-car class reached a new peak with the 1966 Caprice, now a separate series comprising two- and four-door hardtops and a four-door wagon. All featured unique styling touches outside and opulent interiors with simulated woodgrain trim and either plush cloth or all-vinyl upholstery. Bucket front seats and shift console were available, as highlighted here.

With its upper-class appointments and friendly Chevy prices, Caprice was a strong seller for 1966, attracting some 181,000 valuewise shoppers.

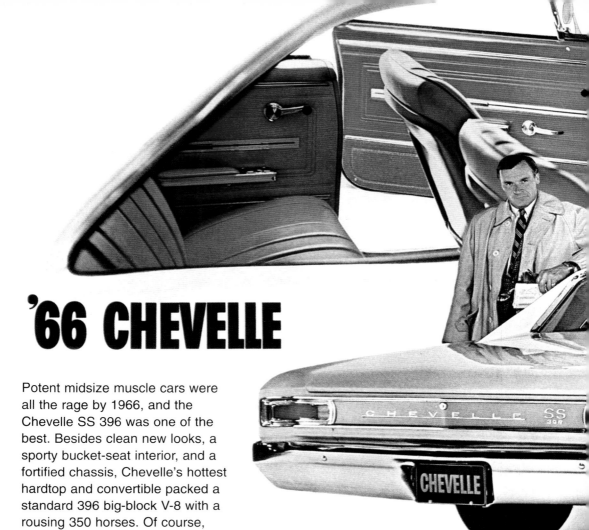

'66 CHEVELLE

Potent midsize muscle cars were all the rage by 1966, and the Chevelle SS 396 was one of the best. Besides clean new looks, a sporty bucket-seat interior, and a fortified chassis, Chevelle's hottest hardtop and convertible packed a standard 396 big-block V-8 with a rousing 350 horses. Of course, owners who knew how were quick to tune it up for even more muscle.

'67

A major restyle gave 1967 full-size Chevrolets an artful blend of creases, bulges, and curves. Top-line Caprice hardtops, like this four-door, might be mistaken for Cadillacs with their standard vinyl roof coverings and optional rear fender skirts. Interiors were more luxurious than ever—and roomier too, thanks to a new swept-back instrument panel that opened up extra leg and knee room in front. Engine options ranged up to a new 427 V-8 with a stout 385 horsepower.

MAKES ELEGANCE AN EVERYDAY AFFAIR

Corvette styling was cleaner than ever for 1967, the swan song for the classic Sting Ray design. It was faster than ever too, thanks to available big-block 427 V-8s of up to 425 horsepower, good for 0-60 mph in just five seconds or less. Cars so equipped came with a hood scoop.

1968

Chevrolet's new-for-'67 Camaro answered the Ford Mustang ponycar, and was a solid hit itself. Changes were minor for '68. The sporty convertible and hard-top coupe offered a huge choice of options, including a performance-focused SS package and a stylish Rally Sport appearance group.

'68 Chevrolets

Chevrolet tempted buyers for 1968 with (clockwise) refined Camaros, a sexy new Corvette convertible and coupe, larger Chevy II compacts, and sleek redesigned Chevelles. And there were careful updates to full-size Chevrolets, which now included the attractively priced Impala Custom hardtop coupe. So whether you wanted high value, high performance, high luxury, or all three, Chevrolet had a car for you in '68.

The 1968 Corvette had more flash and gadgets than the Sting Ray it replaced, but the same basic chassis and powerteams made it no less the fast, fiery sports car. The redesign brought flow-through ventilation for both coupe (above) and ragtop, plus lift-off roof panels that turned the coupe into a semiconvertible.

1969

Full-size 1969 Chevrolets sported flow-through "Astro Ventilation" that eliminated front-door vent windows. It was part of a burly new look that also featured prominent bulges around the wheels and massive loop-style front and rear bumpers. As ever, the big-Chevy lineup was big itself, ranging from sub-$3000 two-door sedans to near-$4000 top-trim wagons.

Chevelle

Though little-changed from its '68 redesign, the midsize Chevelle notched somewhat higher sales for 1969. Two-doors remained on a shorter wheelbase than four-door Chevelles, but all models found wide buyer approval. Speed demons flocked to the high-performance SS hardtop coupe or convertible, which now offered an optional version of the 396 V-8 with 375 horsepower and truly thrilling acceleration.

Camaro

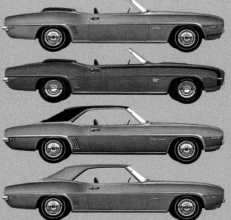

Camaros got a one-year-only restyle for 1969. Left unchanged was a versatile basic design that could be personalized in countless ways with a stroll through the options book. Performance fans were again tempted by muscular SS 350 and SS 396 packages, as well as the racing-inspired Z28 hardtop with a high-winding 302 V-8 and competition-tuned suspension.

Nova

The compact Chevy II was renamed Nova for 1969—and was no longer so compact, having been remodeled as a smaller version of the midsize Chevelle. That meant "more metal for the money," a sales plus. Always popular, Nova offered two- and four-door sedans. Most were sold with family oriented trim, features, and pricing, but hot SS 350 and SS 396 options were available for two-doors.

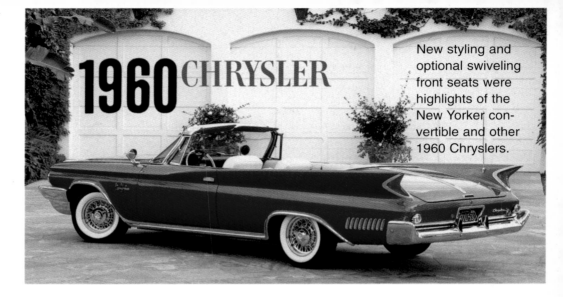

1960 CHRYSLER

New styling and optional swiveling front seats were highlights of the New Yorker convertible and other 1960 Chryslers.

Besides fresh looks, the 1960 Chryslers switched from traditional body-on-frame construction to a welded "Unibody" design. The cars were thus less prone to squeaks and rattles, but somewhat more prone to early rust. A special "cross-hairs" grille marked the rapid 300F hardtop coupe (above) and convertible, which offered up to 400 horsepower.

Chrysler's 1960 styling featured large trapezoidal grilles and soaring tailfins with neat pie-wedge taillamps. Entry-level Windsors and midrange Saratogas (above and below left) used a fine-checked grille. Premium New Yorkers (below center and right) had thin bars slightly recessed. Chrysler sales picked up a bit with the all-new 1960 design.

1961

100

Chrysler revised appearances for 1961 by inverting grilles, slanting the quad headlamps, and remodeling rear ends. Most critics felt the result was less cohesive than 1960 styling. But Chrysler scored big with Newport, a new lower-priced base series starting at just $2964, a bona fide bargain for a big, posh Detroit automobile. Buyers responded to Newport's value story in a still-difficult economy, and Chrysler sales improved to over 96,000, the best tally in several years. By contrast, demand for top-line New Yorkers remained weak. The hardtop coupe (left) drew just 2541 orders, the glamorous convertible (above) a mere 576. Continued were such established Chrysler hallmarks as torsion-bar front suspension and pushbutton-controlled TorqueFlite automatic transmission. Also returing was the high-performance Chrysler, this year named 300G, which accounted for only 1617 sales.

1962

After years as Detroit's prime exponent of tailfins, Chrysler shaved them off for 1962. Historians later called these facelifted cars the "plucked chickens." With growing buyer interest in sportier cars, Chrysler replaced its midrange line with "nonletter" 300 models. They proved popular, offering the style and most of the sizzle of the limited-edition 300s for much less money.

1963

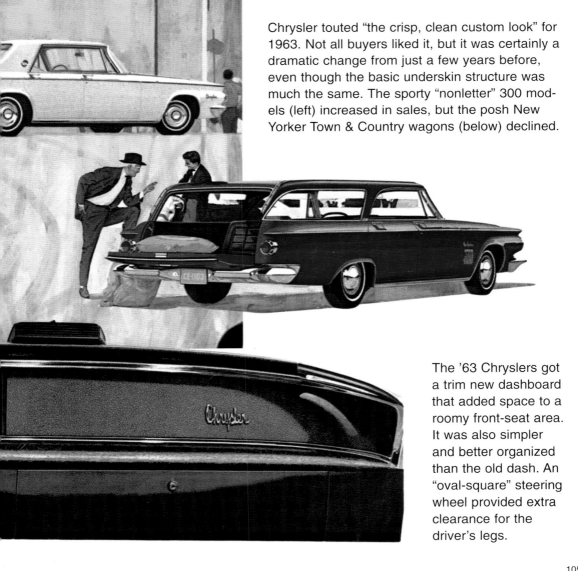

Chrysler touted "the crisp, clean custom look" for 1963. Not all buyers liked it, but it was certainly a dramatic change from just a few years before, even though the basic underskin structure was much the same. The sporty "nonletter" 300 models (left) increased in sales, but the posh New Yorker Town & Country wagons (below) declined.

The '63 Chryslers got a trim new dashboard that added space to a roomy front-seat area. It was also simpler and better organized than the old dash. An "oval-square" steering wheel provided extra clearance for the driver's legs.

1964

The 1964 Chryslers got a light restyle with modest blades on the rear fenders that suggested tail-fins. But it was only a suggestion. Chrysler knew big fins were now a thing of the past. Wide red-white-and-blue "star" ornaments identified the popular midline 300 models, as shown here.

1965

Redesigned from road to roof, the 1965 Chryslers set a new sales record for the brand in what was Detroit's peak sales year of the decade. Many felt this styling was some of Chrysler's best: clean, simple, elegant. Interestingly, the cars looked longer, but were actually a bit shorter than before, though no less spacious inside. Slightly bulged sides contrasted nicely with flat hood and deck lines, as on the 300 model above.

After 10 years as the limited-edition high-performance Chrysler, the "letter-series" 300 came to an end with 1965's 300L. It was mainly done in by the far more popular and profitable "nonletter" 300s. Only 2845 of the L models were built, including 2405 hardtop coupes (below) and just 440 convertibles. All are collector's items today.

1966

Chrysler sales went still higher for 1966. Freshened styling helped. So did a big new 440 V-8 with up to 350 horses The brawny "TNT" was optional for low-line Newports like the convertible in this ad. The text touts the "safety of legendary Chrysler engineering," plus several safety features that were actually government-required for all cars. But Chrysler still had a trump card in an industry-exclusive 5-year/50,000-mile powertrain warranty, which occasioned some fine print at the end of most ads.

CHRYSLER DIVISION ◆ CHRYSLER MOTORS CORPORATION

**Youth is a state of mind.
Chrysler is built for it.**

The one big car built to match the excitement of youth is the 1966 Chrysler.

It's styled with a purposeful look. Its lines are clean. No excess ornamentation.

The new optional 440 TNT V-8 matches in action what is so apparent in looks. It is the biggest passenger car engine we have ever built.

To complement Chrysler's new performance capability is the safety of Chrysler's legendary engineering.

Included as standard equipment are safety-action door handles, Safety-Rim wheels, padded instrument panel and sun visors, seat belts and the protection of Chrysler's exclusive 5-year/50,000-mile engine and drive train warranty.* See your Chrysler dealer.

Move up to Chrysler... it's easy.

*CHRYSLER'S 5-YEAR/50,000-MILE WARRANTY WITH THIS COVERAGE: Chrysler Corporation warrants, for 5 years or 50,000 miles, whichever comes first, against defects in materials and workmanship and will replace or repair at a Chrysler Motors Corporation Authorized Dealer's place of business, without charge for required parts and labor, the engine block, head and internal parts, intake manifold, water pump, transmission case and internal parts (excluding manual clutch), torque converter, drive shaft, universal joints, rear axle and differential, and rear wheel bearings of its 1966 automobiles, provided the owner has the engine oil changed every 3 months or 4,000 miles, whichever comes first, the oil filter replaced every second oil change and the carburetor air filter cleaned every 6 months and replaced every 2 years, and every 6 months furnishes to such a dealer evidence of performance of the required service, and requests the dealer to certify (1) receipt of such evidence and (2) the car's then current mileage.

CHRYSLER

There are many logical reasons for buying a Chrysler. But if you feel great all over when you look at one, who cares about logic?

After all, did anyone ask whether Venus was a good cook? So if you buy a car strictly on looks . . . look.

After you've looked, read what follows.

Chrysler has had the reputation of being a big, expensive automobile.

It's still big.

But five (full-size) Chrysler Newports are priced just a few dollars a month more than the most popular smaller cars, comparably equipped.

This includes the cost of power steer-ing, power brakes, a big V-8, automatic transmission, radio and standard items like safety door handles and seat belts.

Now, how do you personalize this much car? Newport lets you pick from 376 color and trim combinations.

Move up to Chrysler. It's easy.

CHRYSLER

Another ad from Chrysler's 1967 campaign pictures a 300 hardtop coupe, but mostly extols the big-car value of entry-level Newport models. Chrysler had been pressing that point since Newport's 1961 debut, prom-ising "no junior edi-tions" even as rival brands went in for lower-priced com-pacts. Chrysler's strategy had merit, but was ultimately less successful in sales terms. Even so, Chrysler stuck to its guns and kept on promoting more car for the money. One result was slo-gans like "Move up to Chrysler. It's easy." And in the late 1960s at least, many buyers did.

111

1967

New lower-body styling gave 1967 Chryslers a sculpted appearance. Hardtop coupes also got a jaunty semifastback roofline. Each series still had its own frontend look, with a pointy beak unique to 300s like the one in this ad. Note the more emphatic '67 ad slogan. In another highly popular move, Chrysler added Newport Custom models with more standard features but only slightly higher prices than regular Newports.

Chrysler 300:
a special car for special people.

Special in the way it looks.

Clean-lined. With a personality all its own.

Special in the way it moves.

With the biggest standard engine in the price class. And the biggest brakes to go along with it.

Special in what it's got. Standard equipment that's optional on most other cars.

The most copied automatic transmission in the business comes at no extra cost, for example.

So do contoured bucket seats.

And a racing-type torsion bar suspension system.

Chrysler 300.

It's got what it takes to Take Charge. Do you?

Take Charge...Move up to Chrysler '67

A hardtop coupe was available in each of Chrysler's four 1967 series; the 300 version is shown above. That year's wagon, however, came only in entry-level Newport trim (below), though it retained the Town & Country name Chrysler had used on its wagons for many years. As ever, simulated woodgrain side paneling was a popular option.

1968

Maybe your favorite chair should be in your car.

No two people are alike. That includes you. So we offer a variety of seats in our New Yorker.

The 3-in-1 divided front seat—a highly versatile piece of furniture. Armrest up, it's over five feet wide. Armrest down, you get the feel of real buckets. And

the seats adjust individually. For additional comfort, the passenger's side reclines.

Contoured bucket seats are another way to go. They're anthropometrically designed. That means custom comfort. They're shaped to fit you. No matter what shape you're in. Then, there's our standard New Yorker

seat. Deep coil springs. Not one, but two layers of padding. And 9-inch-wide pull-down center armrests both front and rear.

If your favorite chair isn't in your car today, it can be—tomorrow. Make your move.

MOVE UP TO CHRYSLER

CHRYSLER

New Yorker 4-Door Hardtop

The 1968 Chryslers were visually updated with new grilles, trim, and tail styling. Hidden headlamps concealed behind flip-up grille doors were a new feature for 300s like the convertible shown above. As a midseason sales booster, Chrysler offered wagonlike "Sportsgrain" side trim as an option for the Newport hardtop coupe (left) and convertible. It was an interesting idea, but attracted very few customers. Small side-marker lights in the rear fenders and front-bumper ends were among several new federally required safety features appearing on all 1968 cars, foreign and domestic.

Your next car: The great new Chrysler

CHRYSLER

Announcing your next car:

The great new Chrysler.

CHRYSLER

1969

Chrysler billed its 1969 offerings as "Your Next Car," but drew somewhat fewer buyers than the previous model year. That surely disappointed Chrysler dealers, because the '69s were fully redesigned with curved "fuselage styling," marked by smoothly bulged sides and large bumper/grille combinations. Helped by lower rooflines, the new models appeared more massive. And they were. Length stretched to nearly 19 feet, width to almost seven feet—as big as American cars would ever get. Of course, Chrysler wasn't alone in such "supersizing." Other Detroit cars also packed on inches and pounds as the 1960s drew to a close—and for a good reason: Most buyers seemed to want it. Still, the added length did little, if anything, for '69 Chrysler interior space, though these big bruisers were already very roomy. Posh, too.

The burly 300 convertible
was the rarest of all 1969
Chryslers. Just 1933
were built. Convertible
sales were by now on the
wane all over Detroit,
mainly due to the ragtop's
added cost and inconven-
ience—and ever-cheaper
air conditioning for steel-
top models.

1960 De Soto

DeSoto followed most other 1960 Chrysler Corporation cars in switching from traditional body-on-frame construction to a stronger new "unibody" design. But DeSotos were less distinctive than they had been, a reflection of steadily falling sales. The 1960 models, in fact, were little more than retrimmed Chrysler sedans and hardtops, offered in Fireflite and uplevel Adventurer versions. DeSoto's instrument panel was less "space age" than Chrysler's, but both makes offered jazzy swiveling front seats as a new option.

DS-1960

Adventurer

Nothing says Quality like the 1960 De Soto

DeSoto was also denied a trunklid with a dummy spare tire, as available on some 1960 Chryslers, but that wouldn't have helped sales anyway. The year's top engine option was a burly 383 V-8 with "dual ram induction" and 330 horsepower (above left). DeSoto sold 26,021 of its 1960 models, a far cry from the levels of just a few years before.

1961

DeSoto returned for 1961 with just two- and four-door hardtops a single trim level and one engine—plus a rather debatable facelift. By this time, a changing market was fast squeezing DeSoto out of its narrow price niche. Chrysler recognized this, and ended DeSoto production in late 1960 after 33 years. Just 3034 of the '61s were built.

DODGE
1960

Dodge more than doubled its model-year sales for 1960, thanks largely to that year's new Dart lineup of full-size sedans, hardtops, wagons and convertibles (inset photos). Darts offered six-cylinder and V-8 models with jazzy styling and prices from a low $2300 up to around $3000.

Besides the new low-priced Darts, Dodge delivered more-luxurious cars for 1960, called Matador and Polara. Both series included sedans, hardtops, and wagons. Polaras like this hardtop sedan had extra trim, more features, and higher prices.

1961

After switching to "unibody" construction for 1960, Dodge altered styling for '61, marked by unusual "reverse" tailfins. Mainstream Darts returned in three series and closely resembled top-line Polaras, now the sole upscale line. The main visual differences involved side trim and the low-set wraparound taillamps used on nonwagon Darts. Dart wagons and all Polaras had "jet-tube" taillights, but only Polara offered a hardtop wagon without middle roof pillars. Dodge sales dropped 25 percent in a tough model year.

For 1961, Dodge joined Detroit's swing to compacts with Lancer, a retrimmed version of Chrysler-Plymouth Division's year-old Valiant. Ads stressed the advantages of its "unibody" construction, as on most other Chrysler Corporation cars. Despite that, plus lively enough performance and a fairly broad lineup, Lancer proved a sales disappointment at under 75,000 for the model year. Shown here is the top-trim 770 sedan.

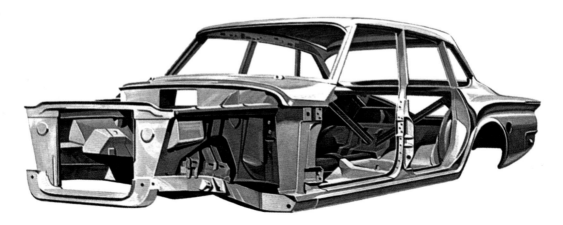

Correcting a major marketing mistake, Dodge revived a true full-size car during 1962 with Custom 880 models (shown) and a lower-priced 880 series. These were basically just the big '61 Dodges shorn of tailfins, but they provided vital sales support at a time when other Dodges didn't appeal that much to buyers.

LOTS OF CAR FOR THE MAN WHO LIKES HIS CAR BIG

Dodge gambled for 1962 by radically shrinking its full-size cars. Sales plunged, a decline helped along by the models' odd new styling. Still, the cars were lighter, so performance and fuel economy improved. The lineup featured mainstream Darts and sporty Polara 500s, including the ragtop shown here.

Lancer
got minor trim
changes for 1962, but
also a spiffy new GT
hardtop (bottom). Besides
a larger 225 "Slant Six"
engine with 145 horsepower,
the GT came with an all-vinyl
bucket-seat interior. Buyers
could choose a manual
transmission with sporty
floorshift or pushbutton
"TorqueFlite" auto-
matic.

1963

Seeking to recover from 1962, Dodge made its "standard" cars a little longer for '63, as well as more conventional looking, though the front end remained debatable. They were offered with six-cylinder and V-8 power in 220, 330, 440, and posh Polara trim, plus V-8 Polara 500s with bucket seats as shown here. Available 413 and 426 "wedgehead" V-8s made these still relatively lightweight cars a power to reckon with in dragstrip racing—and on the street.

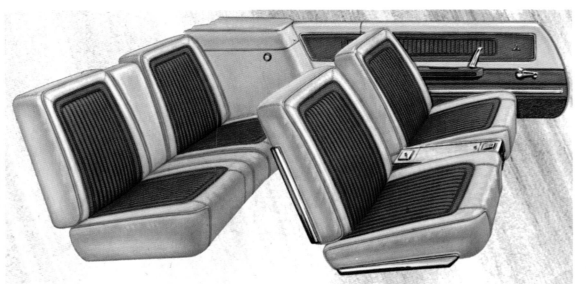

Dart

880

Left: Dart denoted Dodge's 1963 compact, a larger all-new design that proved quite popular with its clean looks and peppy yet frugal Slant Six engines. While most buyers chose a sedan or wagon, Dart also offered rakish hardtops and a top-line GT convertible. Meanwhile, Dodge restyled its big 880 and Custom 880s, shown above and below.

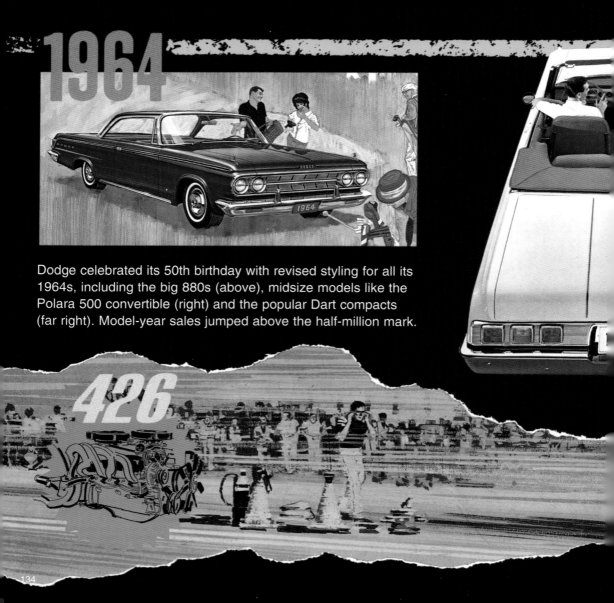

1964

Dodge celebrated its 50th birthday with revised styling for all its 1964s, including the big 880s (above), midsize models like the Polara 500 convertible (right) and the popular Dart compacts (far right). Model-year sales jumped above the half-million mark.

426

Like many rivals, Dodge was really into high performance by 1964. Potent "ram-induction" 413 and 426 wedgehead V-8s with up to 425 horses remained factory available for midsize models, some of which dominated drag racing under the Ramchargers banner.

1965

Handsome new full-size Dodges bowed for 1965 in Polara and Custom 880 trim with a wide choice of V-8 engines. Flagship of the line was the Monaco two-door hardtop (below) with its own buckets-and-console interior.

Midsize Dodges were nicely restyled for 1965 and tagged Coronet, reviving a 1950s Dodge name. The line comprised sedans and hardtop coupes, plus wagons in base, Deluxe, 440, and sporty bucket-seat 500 trim levels. All could be formidable performers with V-8 options up to a 425-horsepower 426 "wedge."

Dodge also restyled its Dart compacts for 1965, but the big news was a first-time V-8 option, an efficient 273 cubic-incher delivering a lively 180 horsepower. It was just the thing for the top-line GT hardtop or convertible, which offered a sporty floorshift for both the automatic and manual transmissions.

1966

Headlining the 1966 Dodge lineup were the luxury Monaco series (above) and all-new midsize Coronets available with an awesome "Street Hemi" V-8.

CORONET

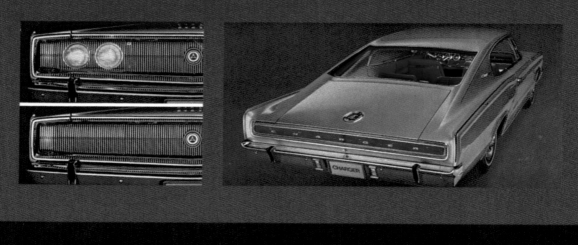

Buyers were showing interest in sloped-roof "fast-back" models by 1966, and Dodge had one of the year's nicest in its new Charger. Though based on the Coronet, it featured its own rakish roofline, exclusive hideaway headlamps, and a special interior with full-length center console and four bucket seats. The rear seats could be flipped down to form a long load deck. Most '66 Chargers used a 383 V-8, but a few were equipped with the new 426 Street Hemi, conservatively rated at 425 hp.

Dodge Charger

DODGE DIVISION ⬥ **CHRYSLER** MOTORS CORPORATION

Ads urged you to "Join the Dodge Rebellion" in 1967. Leading the charge were sporty Coronet 500s (far left) and new R/T "muscle" models with a burly new 440 big-block V-8 as standard. For full-size-car buyers, Dodge had redesigned Polara, sporty Polara 500 (above left) and luxury Monaco models with crisp, sculpted styling. Hardtop coupes sported a jaunty semifastback roofline (below)

1968

Backing up 1968's "Dodge Fever" ad theme was a squadron of fast, flashy models, including a new Dart GTS hardtop (below) with standard 340-cubic-inch V-8 (far right). Equally exciting was an all-new Charger with its curvy hardtop body and slick "tunnelback" roofline, plus available R/T performance equipment. Hot models like these could be ordered with "bumblebee" tail stripes as members of Dodge's "Scat Pack."

What's striped for action   ...built for comfort   ...and has a lot of dash?

Charger R/T...the only car that looks as good as it goes.

Dodge · CHRYSLER

No wonder Charger sales are up more than 250%* over last year's. Where else can you get a shape you can tell a block away, hidden headlights, deep foam buckets in luxurious deep-pleated vinyl, and that great-looking dash with the readable dials? Not to mention an electric clock that really works, a racing gas cap, and handy door pockets for maps and things. Plus that combination of agility and comfort that's hard to match.

The car shown above is an R/T—in our new spring color, Charger Green Metallic. In Dodge lingo, R/T means you get a 440 Magnum V8, special rallye suspension, oversized police-type brakes, and your choice of shiftable three-speed automatic or four-on-the-floor, all at no extra cost. Which, all added up, means just about the greatest piece of machinery on four wheels. About the bumblebee stripes: Whether or not they

go on your R/T is up to you.

Options? Air conditioning, 8-track stereo-tape player, Auto Pilot speed control, rear window defogger—the works. But you'll still pay less for a car equipped the way you want because more of the things you want are standard equipment.

Satisfied with a 250% sales increase? Good heavens, sir! We haven't even warmed up yet.

*Retail year as of March 1, 1968.

DODGE fever

145

1969

Dodge again played up its "Scat Pack" performance cars for 1969, including (from top) Charger R/T, Coronet R/T, Coronet Super Bee, and Dart GTS. The Super Bee was Dodge's "budget" muscle car, packing a potent 335-horse 383 "Magnum" V-8, plus a firm suspension and fat tires on styled wheels. Dodge remained a power in stock-car racing and on the drag strips.

CHARGER R/T

CORONET R/T HARDTOP

SUPER BEE HARDTOP

DART GTSPORT HARDTOP

Run with the Dodge Scat Pack

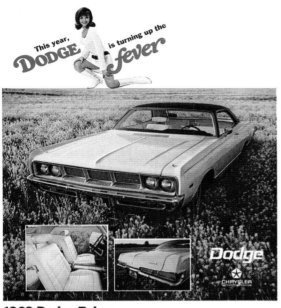

1969 Dodge Polara.
Totally new, it is. Expensive, it isn't.

If you're looking for a big, luxurious new car that sports a low price, look no farther. 1969 Dodge Polara. With such standard items as foam-padded seats, carpeting, and a 230-hp V8. Not to mention an all-new instrument panel and concealed windshield wipers. Why wait, big car lovers? This is your year. 1969 Dodge Polara.

Full-size Dodges were redesigned for 1969, gaining curvy "fuselage" styling that looked good but added inches and pounds. Though Monacos remained the brand's luxury flagships, Polaras were promoted as good value in what we might now call a "near-luxury" car. Engines, all V-8s, ran the gamut from a mild base 318 to a big-block Magnum 440 with 375 horses. To make sure John Law could keep pace, Dodge continued offering a special police package for Polara with a heavy-duty powertrain and chassis.

147

EDSEL

A spectacular sales flop in 1958-59, Edsel returned for its third season as basically a retrimmed version of the all-new 1960 full-size Ford. But the name was a national joke and beyond saving, so Edsel was dropped in late 1959 after just 2846 of the '60s were built. This Ranger four-door sedan was the best-seller at 1288 units.

Edsel ended its brief life as Ford Motor Company's "young executive" brand with Ranger sedans, hard-tops, and convertible, plus two Villager wagons. The last saw combined pro-duction of just 275 units.

149

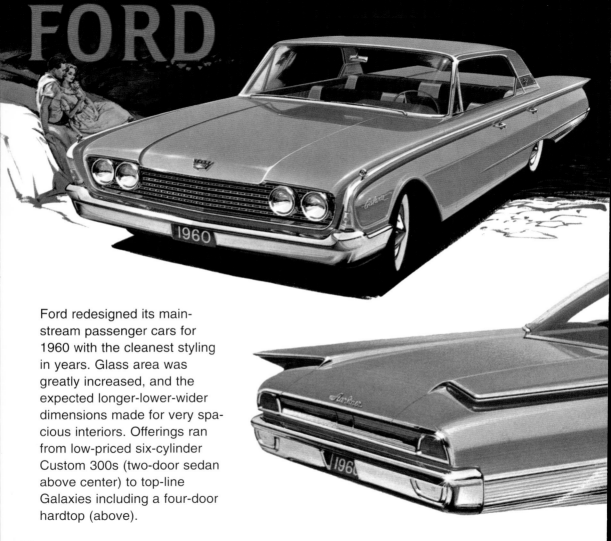

FORD

1960

Ford redesigned its main-
stream passenger cars for
1960 with the cleanest styling
in years. Glass area was
greatly increased, and the
expected longer-lower-wider
dimensions made for very spacious interiors. Offerings ran
from low-priced six-cylinder
Custom 300s (two-door sedan
above center) to top-line
Galaxies including a four-door
hardtop (above).

1960 *a wonderful new world*

Though most Galaxies retained a squared-off rear roofline, the 1960 line added an attractive sloped-rear-roof hardtop coupe called Starliner. It was moderately popular with 68,461 sold.

Ford Falcon

Ford's Falcon was by far the most popular of the Big Three's new 1960 compacts—a modern Model A. At the other end of the spectrum, Ford's Thunderbird offered sporty luxury for four.

Thunderbird

1961 Thunderbird

Thunderbird was new from road to roof for 1961, and striking from any angle. A new feature for both the coupe and convertible was the novel "Swing-Away" steering wheel (below), which made for easier entry and exit in Ford's low-slung luxury liners. A smooth 300-horsepower 390-cubic-inch V-8 was standard.

Falcon eschewed major changes and remained a hot seller for 1961. Joining sedans and wagons with two and four doors was a sporty Futura two-door with front bucket seats.

All standard Fords were nicely restyled for 1961. They included the high-value Fairlanes and Fairlane 500s (below right), Galaxie square-roof and Starliner hardtops (below) and woody-look Country Squire wagon.

155

'62

Ford hit a sales home run with a new 1962 Fairlane (below and upper left). Resized midway between standard Fords and the compact Falcon (left), Fairlane offered sedans and wagons with a sturdy six-cylinder base engine (above right). Optional were lively new 221 and 260 "Challenger" V-8s with up to 164 horses.

Thunderbird added a dashing
Sports Roadster for 1962
(opposite, top). It was basically the
regular convertible with genuine
wire wheels and a rear-seat cover
to give the appearance of a two-
seat sports car. Today, it's a highly
prized collector's item. The '62
full-size Fords (other photos) got
fresh styling, plus new Galaxie
500XL models with front bucket
seats and center console. Also
new was an available 406 V-8
with up to 425 horsepower.

1963

Ford touted many "Better Ideas" for 1963, starting with a posh Limited Edition Landau hardtop for Thunderbird (above). Full-size models were restyled and dubbed the "Super Torque" Fords. Top-line Galaxie 500XLs (below) offered burly new 427 V-8 options packing up to 425 horsepower. Falcon now offered hardtops (upper right) and convertibles, including sporty V-8 Sprints, plus the usual sedans and wagons. The midsize Fairlane also added hardtops, including a bucket-seat Sport Coupe.

1964

Ford said all its 1964s offered "Total Performance." Full-size models boasted fresh looks, plus new features like thin-shell bucket seats (below).

Falcon got its first major restyle for 1964. The V-8 Sprint convertible (top right) remained the sportiest of Ford's compacts. Midsize Fairlanes like the 500 Sport Coupe (middle right) were also freshened, but maintained a visual link with big Fords. Though still "Unique in All the World," Thunderbird was redesigned for '64, gaining a more-chiseled look and new gadgets without greatly changing size or underskin components. "Lounge" rear seats were among the highlights.

1965

Ford redesigned its full-size cars for 1965 with a crisp, semiformal look. The Galaxie line again listed a sporty 500XL convertible (bottom), plus posh new LTD hardtops claimed to be "quieter than a Rolls-Royce." Falcons were mildly updated for '65 (Squire wagon below), while midsize Fairlanes (right) adopted square-rigged lines.

How it feels to take off in a Fairlane. You feel the thrust of Fairlane's 289 cu. in. V-8 option—the engine that Cobra-builder Carroll Shelby calls "the best ever to come out of Detroit." You feel the solid quality of the car— a quality that is proved by millions of owner-driven miles. And you feel the solid contentment of a man who's made a *buy.* Can all this be true? You bet! *Ask any Fairlane owner.*

FORD

Thunderbird received modest trim changes for 1965, plus taillights with sequential turn signals. Shown here is the year's new Limited Edition Special Landau hardtop with all-vinyl parchment interior and matching vinyl top, plus "Ember-Glo" metallic paint.

Ford came up with Detroit's biggest success of the decade when the Mustang bowed in April 1964 with hardtop and convertible models. A slick "2+2" fast-back coupe (near left) was added at the start of the '65 model year. Though based on the humble Falcon, this sporty new compact offered high style at low cost, plus enough options to satisfy any buyer. No wonder Ford sold more than a million "ponycars" in the long debut model year—a first-season sales record that still stands. A legend had been born.

1966

Ford focused on midsize cars for 1966, issuing redesigned Fairlanes with much curvier styling and enough underhood room for rip-snorting big-block V-8s. The most-popular models were the uplevel Fairlane 500s, which included (from top) a standard two-door hardtop, stylish Squire wagon, and sporty XL GT convertible.

Mustang sales remained red-hot in 1966, helped by revised engine choices with more power, deft styling enhancements, and new optional features. Meanwhile, Ford played up the luxury of its big LTDs by briefly offering a special-order "stretch" conversion of the 1966 four-door hardtop (below). It carried the normal factory warranty but cost a mint, so few were built.

A new option for '66 Thunderbirds was the Town Hardtop roof (above). It created some awful blind spots. For more-practical folk, Ford offered redesigned Falcons, including a spiffy Futura Sport Coupe two-door and a Ranchero pickup.

1967

Mustang galloped into 1967 with huskier styling and optional big-block V-8s among the changes. Thunderbird was redesigned to be larger and more luxurious than ever. Bigger still was the new T-Bird sedan with center-opening doors (right). It replaced the convertible. All '67 T-Birds hid their headlamps in a massive bumper/grille.

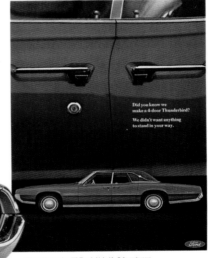

Did you know we make a 4-door Thunderbird?

We didn't want anything to stand in your way.

That's why we make a '67 Thunderbird with all the excitement of Thunderbird styling plus four doors for handy entering, exiting. Once again this year, Thunderbird is unique. The model with four center-opening doors, inspired by Lincoln Continental, is the one personal luxury car with this convenience. The two-door '67 Thunderbird is as singular—as breathtakingly personal —as ever. The way for you to go is clear. See your Ford Dealer.

Thunderbird
Unique in all the world

1967

SelectAire Conditioner

"Tailored Tires"

SelectShift Cruise-O-Matic

Convenience Control Panel

Stereo-Sonic Tape System with AM F

Full-size Fords were also redesigned for 1967. Every model benefited from sleeker lines, especially sportier versions like the Galaxie 500XL convertible. Included on the options list were air conditioning, wider tires, sporty "Select-Shift" automatic transmission, extra warning lights, AM/FM stereo radio, and 8-track stereo tape player.

Fingertip Speed Control

Wagon Magic Doorgate

SHOW YOUR STRIPES!

That GT feeling is contagious: every Fairlane owner has it.

And every Fairlane owner knows it. The feeling that comes with driving a car that was built to perform. And gives you the luxury you've always wanted. Like Stereo Tape. Engines up to 427 cu. in. Air Conditioning. Show your stripes! Pick your Fairlane sedan, hardtop, convertible, or wagon – soon! **FAIRLANE**

Other big-Ford features for '67 included optional "Fingertip Speed Control," with handy steering-wheel buttons, and a two-way "Magic Doorgate" for wagons that both swung to the side and flipped down. Fairlane fought for Ford in Detroit's raging muscle car war with available 390 and 427 big-block V-8s that also won big in stock-car racing.

1968

Midsize Fords were again redesigned for '68, with a new Torino convertible pacing that year's Indy 500 (inset). Hidden headlamps were a new styling touch on the Galaxie 500XL (shown) and LTD.

The 1968 Mustangs and Thunderbirds focused on meeting the federal government's new safety and emissions standards, so appearance changed little on both. Continuing a line of special high-performance Mustangs were Carroll Shelby's V-8 GT-350 and big-block GT-500 fastbacks and convertibles (below), all with unique racing-inspired styling and equipment.

1969

A cleaner-running 429 V-8 option highlighted 1969 refinements for the flagship LTD (above) and other full-size Fords. That year's midsize Fairlane line reprised a racy fastback that was newly available in high-performance Torino Cobra trim (below). Its standard 428 was deliberately underrated at 335 horses.

An optional power sliding sunroof led a short list of changes for the '69 Thunderbirds (right). Mustangs were revamped for '69 to be the biggest and brawniest yet. Bringing racetrack excitement to the showroom was a new Boss 302 fastback (below) with a high-winding 302 V-8. It also boasted unique styling touches such as front and rear spoilers and "hockey stick" side stripes, plus ultra-firm suspension, fat tires, bigger brakes, and quick-ratio steering.

the exclusive

IMPERIAL
AMERICA'S MOST CAREFULLY BUILT CAR

Chrysler Corporation's luxury flagship, from the late 1950s through the early '60s, was promoted and manufactured as an independent brand. All Imperials used a 350-horsepower 413 V-8 and Chrysler's pushbutton "TorqueFlite" automatic transmission.

1961

Imperial's tailfins grew taller with the 1961 models, which also sported a new "face" with 1930s-style freestanding headlights. The midrange Crown series offered these Southampton hardtops at $5500-$5600. Entry-level Custom versions cost about $500 less.

With buyers tired of tailfins, Imperial's rear fenders were planed flat for 1962 and topped by "gun-sight" taillamps. New in front were a stand-up hood ornament and a divided grille. This is the top-line LeBaron hardtop sedan.

A new grille insert and taillamps nestled in reshaped rear fenders marked 1963 Imperials like this Crown Southampton 4-door hardtop. But little else was new, so Chrysler's flagship line remained in a sales slump, running a distant third to newer designs from Big Three rivals Cadillac and Lincoln.

1964

Imperial sales jumped to their highest mark of the decade for 1964, thanks to a full redesign by the same stylist who designed the 1961 Lincoln. The Crown series included this convertible and 2-door hardtop.

1965

The 1965 Imperials received subtle visual changes, mostly at the front. The Crown convertible remained the line's only ragtop—and the least-popular model, with just 633 built for '65. Here it fronts the most-popular offering, the Crown hardtop sedan, which drew 11,628 sales this year. All Imperials still used a 413-cubic-inch V-8, but the mandatory automatic transmission switched from pushbuttons to a conventional lever control.

1966

A big new 440-cube V-8 provided 350 horses for 1966 Imperials, which received another round of detail styling alterations. Imperial still easily matched its Detroit rivals for convenience gadgets and classy cabin comfort, yet overall sales were down for '65 and slumped again for '66 to fewer than 13,750. The elegant Crown convertible shown here drew a mere 514 buyers.

1967

In a money-saving move prompted by declining sales, Imperial returned to its roots for 1967, being redesigned as basically a more luxurious Chrysler on the same unibody platform. But the change from body-on-frame construction did reduce weight, which improved performance and fuel economy, and Imperials had their own styling on a longer wheelbase than Chrysler's. This LeBaron hardtop sedan was priced close to $6700, the costliest offering in a lineup that was thinned to five models.

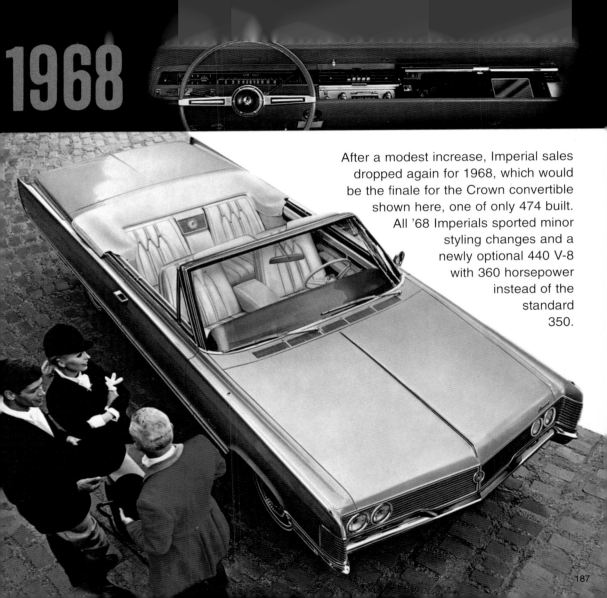

1968

After a modest increase, Imperial sales dropped again for 1968, which would be the finale for the Crown convertible shown here, one of only 474 built. All '68 Imperials sported minor styling changes and a newly optional 440 V-8 with 360 horsepower instead of the standard 350.

1969

  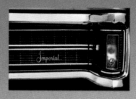

Along with its Chrysler parent, Imperial was redesigned for 1969 with billowy new "fuselage" styling. The flagships had their own hidden-headlamp grille and rear end, plus a standard 440-cubic-inch V-8 and Chrysler Corporation's best interior trim. Models again numbered five, including the uplevel LeBaron hardtop sedan (below) and the entry-level Crown two-door hardtop (inset). Imperial's convertible body style was retired.

189

Typical of 1960 luxury-car ads, this Lincoln spread used stylish artwork instead of photos to glamorize its styling and top-quality interiors.

Lincoln

LINCOLN FOR 1960

Like rival Cadillac, Lincoln began
the 1960s by reprising its 1959
design with only detail changes.
This is the premiere Landau
hardtop sedan. These were among
the world's most extravagant cars,
at almost 19 feet long and weighing
some 6000 pounds. All used a
430-cubic-inch V-8.

1961

Lincoln broke dramatically from its recent past with a smaller, all-new Continental for 1961. The previous three-series line-up was replaced by just two models: this four-door sedan and America's first four-door convertible in a decade. Both featured rear-hinged back doors and clean, tailored styling that was honored with an award from the Industrial Design Institute. Built with care and backed by a longer-than-usual warranty, as this ad proclaims, the '61 Continental halted a four-year Lincoln sales slide.

The new Continental convertible stowed its fabric top beneath the rear deck for an ultraclean look. It wasn't cheap at over $6700, versus $6000 for the sedan, but it was arguably the most glamorous American car of 1961.

The critical and commercial success of the 1961 Continental established a basic design theme that Lincoln would rely on for the next 25 years. Interior design took inspiration from the "modern-classic" Continental Mark II of 1956-57, but was 1960s-contemporary in look and layout. A symmetrically arrayed three-pod instrument panel included central vents and climate controls beneath a transistorized radio, the newest thing in audio hi-tech.

Some road tests criticized the 1961 Continentals as far less spacious inside than previous Lincolns. Even so, the trimmer new package provided good rear-seat room for two adults—plus easier access to it through the 1930s-style rear-hinged doors. As ever, Lincoln used top-grade fabrics and leather, but workmanship was visibly improved, thanks in part to numerous tests and inspections given each car before delivery.

1962

The handsome Continental returned for 1962 with flush-mounted head-lamps and a new texture for the grille and taillight panel. There were several mechanical improvements too, including larger brakes and oil-change intervals stretched to 30,000 miles. Model-year sales improved to 25,160 units.

1963

Lincoln had announced that the 1961 Continental wouldn't change for the mere sake of change, so refinement was again the keynote for 1963. More minor styling changes occurred, but the big news was a 430-cubic-inch V-8 with a four-barrel carburetor that added 20 horsepower for 320 in all. Engineers also created a bit more trunk space. Lincoln posted another yearly sales increase, reaching 31,233.

FOR 1963, WE HAVE ENLARGED YOUR PRIVATE WORLD AND PROVIDED YOU WITH ADDED POWER

Close the doors...the classic Continental look is little changed for 1963. (One reason this car retains its value.) Then open the doors, and discover the new spaciousness in the passenger compartments. There is greater usable capacity in the luggage compartment, too.

Now, drive the car, and experience the augmented power of the 1963 engine, providing superior acceleration for passing at freeway speeds.

Important changes, but none for the sake of

change. For the only changes we make are functional refinements which add to its quality.

This is the Lincoln Continental for 1963, your finest motorcar investment for the years ahead. And as final proof of quality, the warranty: two full years or 24,000 miles, the longest total-car warranty offered on any American automobile.*

LINCOLN CONTINENTAL
Product of Ford Motor Company Lincoln-Mercury Division

*Ford Motor Company warrants to its dealers, and its dealers, in turn, warrant to their Lincoln Continental customers as follows: That for 24 months or for 24,000 miles, whichever comes first, free replacement, including related labor, will be made by dealers, of any part with a defect in workmanship or materials. Tires are not covered by the warranty; appropriate adjustments will be made by tire companies. Owners will remain responsible for normal maintenance service and routine replacement of items such as filters, spark plugs, ignition points and wiper blades.

1964

Lincoln issued redesigned Continentals for 1964 with three inches added in the midsection to increase rear-seat room. A more subtle change was replacing the previous curved side windows with flat glass, which gave occupants a little more shoulder width. A slightly higher roof increased head room. For all this, designers did not tamper much with the successful Lincoln look. Several new options arrived, including individual power front seats and an adjustable steering column.

ENTER LIKE A LADY

Notice the doors. Four. This is America's only four-door convertible. And notice how they open. From the center, to make everyone's entrances graceful.

Inside, there is greater safety. All four door lock automatically when the driver flicks a single switch. And there is luxury: in fine soft upholstery, rich looped carpeting, exquisite details like the walnut inlay on the glove box and door panels. And there is extra space. This is the only convertible whose rear seat is wide enough for three adults to ride in comfort... wider than in any other convertible.

But great engineering is equally important in the Continental concept. This car is designed and constructed to the highest standards in the world.

Of course, it is costly. But we refuse to compromise and build lower priced models as others do. Because they would not be Continentals. There is only one Continental...timeless in styling, enduring in performance, retaining its high value year after year.

For 1963, enter the private world of Lincoln Continental, the finest car in the world.

LINCOLN CONTINENTAL

Product of Ford Motor Company Lincoln-Mercury Division

Besides slightly crisper lines, Continental's 1964 redesign upgraded wheels and tires from 14 to 15 inches, which made a soft, absorbent ride even more so and were longer-wearing to boot. As before, the sedan accounted for the bulk of sales, outpolling the convertible by about 10 to 1. Price was probably a factor. This year's respective base stickers were some $6300 and $7000. Though still a distant second to Cadillac in sales, Lincoln once again attracted more customers than it had the year before, with close to 36,300 orders for the '64 campaign.

1965

Refinement was the unsurprising watchword for the 1965 Continentals. Besides minor styling changes, the only notable news was the addition of transistorized ignition and four-way hazard flasher lights to the options list. Prices were unchanged, but sales sailed past the 40,000 mark.

This is the Lincoln Continental for 1965: America's most distinguished motorcar. It is the luxury automobile that stands apart from all other cars. It distinguishes you among fine car owners.

A PRODUCT OF Ford MOTOR COMPANY · LINCOLN-MERCURY DIVISION

You will notice refinements in styling for 1965. Yet you will also recognize this luxury motorcar as unmistakably Continental. Unique in its classic look. Singular in its luxury and comfort. Unequaled in its ride. Lasting in its investment value. Built only to the world's highest standards. Available in a deliberately limited edition of models: the classic four-door sedan and America's only four-door convertible. Among luxury cars, there continues to be only one Lincoln Continental. What does your car say about you?

LINCOLN *Continental*

America's most distinguished motorcar.

1966

Lincoln was again redesigned for 1966, adding two inches to wheelbase, five inches to overall length, and an elegant hardtop coupe to the lineup. To cope with the extra mass, Lincoln enlarged its V-8 to 462 cubic inches, good for 340 horsepower. Styling remained elegant and instantly recognized as Continental, but was a bit sportier and curvier, especially on the new two-door. A Continental "star" ornament returned atop the hoods of all models, which offered a newly optional seven-position tilt steering wheel. With all this and prices that were actually reduced, Lincoln sales jumped to nearly 55,000, surpassing the previous all-time high set a decade before.

Lincoln Continental
distinguishes your way of life.

Shown above, the Continental coupé, broadening your invitation to ownership. Also available, the sedan and America's only four-door convertible. For 1966, a new 462 cu. in. engine and a completely new transmission. New luxury options include automatic temperature control system, stereo tape/AM radio, and many others.

Lincoln Continental distinguishes you among fine car owners. It is the luxury motorcar that stands apart from all other cars. As an expression of individuality, good taste, accomplishment. As the reflection of a way of life. Come take a closer look: drive it, experience it, and discover for yourself how close you may be to owning a Continental.

LINCOLN-MERCURY DIVISION

LINCOLN *Continental*
America's most distinguished motorcar.

Looking quite elegant in profile (above), the four-door
sedan remained the most popular Continental for 1966,
drawing nearly 36,000 orders. Besides new exterior
styling, all models boasted a new dashboard that
grouped all gauges and controls in front of the driver.

Continental's new-for-'66 hardtop coupe looked pretty in pink, white, and most any other color. It was the main factor in Lincoln's much-improved model-year sales, attracting nearly 16,000 orders, most, all of it "plus" business. One reason: The hardtop coupe was the most affordable '66 Continental, starting at $5485, $265 below the four-door sedan and a sizable $898 less than the convertible.

1967

Lincoln had little really new to talk about for 1967, so ads resorted to "luxury lifestyle" daydreams like this one, though you needn't be airplane-wealthy to afford the car. And, in fact, prices went up only a little that year. Much of that increase covered added standard features, like a windows-up "Fresh Flow" interior ventilation system, plus new government-required safety equipment including emergency flasher lights, dual-circuit brakes with corrosion-resistant lines, and more interior "crash" padding. Sales declined for a change, falling to about 45,700 for the model year.

What does the Continental life say about you?

It may say that you like to fly your own plane.
It says that you enjoy today's good life and live it with zest.
It says your choice of a luxury motorcar is Lincoln Continental.
In fact, more and more people—like yourself—are turning to Lincoln Continental.
And it's understandable. Our styling is unique and commanding.
The sleek, clean, uncluttered lines set the standard for the entire industry—
and give you an investment of lasting value. Luxury options? Certainly.
An impressive variety so you may tailor your Continental to your individual taste.
If you have yet to discover the 1967 Continental, do so now.
Come live the Continental life.

LINCOLN *Continental*
AMERICA'S MOST DISTINGUISHED MOTORCAR

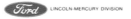

LINCOLN-MERCURY DIVISION

Shown above, the 1967 Continental coupé in Cranberry, with optional black vinyl roof. Also available, the Continental sedan, America's only four-door convertible, and the executive limousine, the ultimate luxury motorcar.

206

1968

The big Continental remained its handsome self for 1968, but lost its "star" hood ornament and slow-selling convertible body style. An impact-absorbing steering column was adopted at Washington's insistence, followed late in the year by a cleaner-running 460 V-8 with 365 horsepower to replace the old-design 462. Lincoln built its millionth car in 1968, but Continental suffered another sales decline, easing to around 39,000 units.

Lincoln's big news for 1968 was the midyear debut of the Continental Mark III, a return to the "personal luxury" idea embodied by the mid-1950s Mark II. Ford Motor Company chairman Henry Ford II was personally involved with the project, which he supported enthusiastically. The Mark III was based on the Ford Thunderbird, though it was hard to tell.

The 1968 Mark III was conceived as a lineal successor to the 1956-57 Mark II. Lincoln stylists made sure people made the connection by giving the new model the same sort of rear-end styling with dummy "Continental" spare, plus rakish long-hood/short-deck pro-portions. New elements included hidden headlamps flanking a square, upright "classic" grille. With its ultraluxurious interior trim and full-boat standard equipment, the Mark III was promoted as no less exclusive than the Mark II and was priced accordingly at $6585—hundreds above the big Lincolns. Even so, it proved a solid sales success, drawing a healthy 7770 orders despite an abbreviated debut model year.

1969

Because it bowed as an "early" 1969 model, the Continental Mark III was virtually unchanged for the formal '69 season, though a few minor parts were swapped out and the starting price raised by $173. Much smaller and somewhat sportier than the big Continentals, the Mark III used the same 460 V-8 and three-speed automatic transmission, so it was a bit quicker and more agile—though hardly a sports car. Demand remained strong as the "true" '69s tallied 23,088 sales.

Senior Continentals returned for 1969 with only detail updates to trim and equipment. Perhaps the biggest visual change was a new grille suggestive of Mercedes-Benz design. Some print advertising, as here, had unusually little to say, perhaps reflecting the old saw about a picture being worth a thousand words, especially with regard to snooty luxury cars. The new Mark III more than offset another big-Lincoln sales dip, and the brand tallied nearly 61,400 orders for the model year.

Lincoln Continental for 1969.

Now more than ever America's most distinguished motorcar. Powered by the incomparable 460 cubic inch V-8 engine. From the Lincoln-Mercury Division of Ford Motor Company.

LINCOLN·MERCURY

MERCURY 1960

Like several rivals, Mercury issued 1960 models that were basically restyled updates of its all-new '59s. The facelift looked especially good on the Montery and Park Lane convertibles.

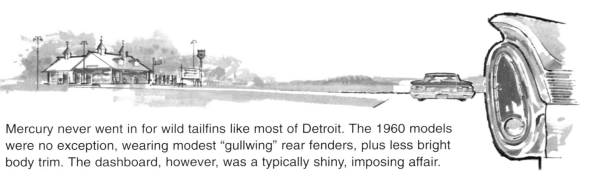

Mercury never went in for wild tailfins like most of Detroit. The 1960 models were no exception, wearing modest "gullwing" rear fenders, plus less bright body trim. The dashboard, however, was a typically shiny, imposing affair.

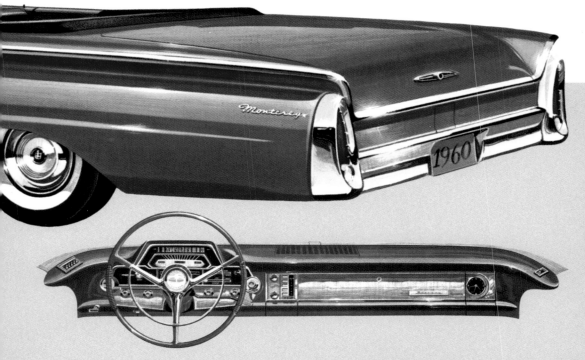

1961

Mercury's traditional medium-price market was dead in the water by 1961. To revive sales, the brand moved into lower-price territory by sharing a platform with Ford for the first time in four years. Supplementing upscale stalwarts like the Colony Park wagon and Monterey convertible were more-affordable new Meteor models including an "800" hardtop coupe (right). The lineup spanned three V-8s offering up to 330 horsepower.

Mercury Super-Economy V-8

Mercury Marauder "352"

Mercury Marauder "390"

215

COMET

Mercury sales got a big boost for 1960 with the compact Comet, essentially a restyled version of Ford's popular Falcon. Only minor changes marked the '61 Comet sedans and wagons, each with two or four doors. Arriving at midyear, however, was a sporty bucket-seat two-door called S-22. Model-year sales jumped from 116,000 to 197,000 for 1961.

Showing another shift in marketing tactics, the "standard" 1962 Mercurys regrouped into Monterey and uplevel Monterey Custom series, plus a parallel wagon lineup headed by a pseudo-wood-trimmed Colony Park. All were still basically "deluxe Fords," so sedans and hardtops got the same new squared-off roofline, but lower-body styling was Mercury's own. A burly 406 V-8 with 385 horses was now the top power option. For all this, big-Merc sales slipped for a second year.

1962

Ford pioneered "midsize" cars with the 1962 Fairlane, and Mercury got its own version that year. Appropriating the Meteor name, these 'tweener' two- and four-door sedans wrapped big-Merc styling cues around a sensible package based on the compact Falcon/Comet. Like Fairlane, Meteor offered a base six-cylinder engine and two light and lively new V-8 options: a 145-horse 221 and a 164-hp 260. Even so, Meteor was far less popular than Fairlane.

1963

The full-size Mercurys got crisp new styling for 1963. Sedans and hardtops featured a novel "Breezeway" rear window with drop-down glass. Flashy S-55 models with bucket seats bowed at midyear.

Besides a minor retrim, Comet added hardtop coupe and convertible models for 1963, plus Meteor's 221 V-8 as a first-time power option. Mercury's compact sales remained strong, but the midsize Meteor languished despite adding its own hardtops (left), including a bucket-seat S-33 model with snazzy interior trim (above).

1964 MERCURY

Mercury turned 25 in 1964, and celebrated by winning 12 stock-car races, five in NASCAR. That year's big-car line offered freshened looks and an optional 427 big-block V-8 with up to 425 hp.

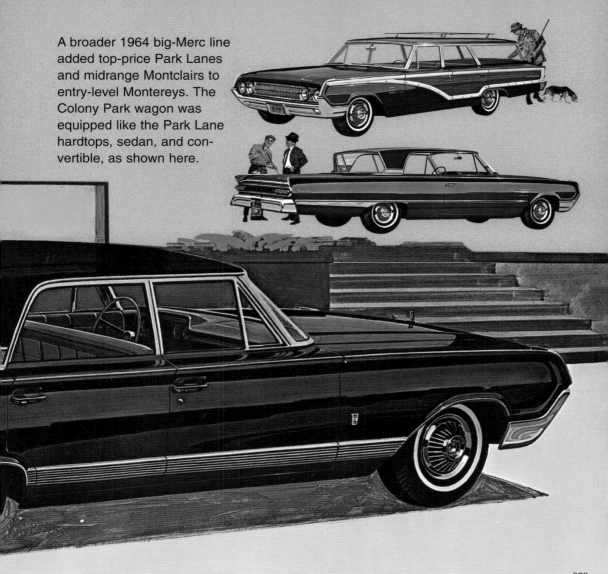

A broader 1964 big-Merc line added top-price Park Lanes and midrange Montclairs to entry-level Montereys. The Colony Park wagon was equipped like the Park Lane hardtops, sedan, and convertible, as shown here.

1964 COMET

Mercury dumped its slow-selling midsize Meteor for 1964. The compact Comet partly filled the gap by growing longer and flashier in its first major makeover. A new top-line Caliente series included Comet's only convertible. Mercury touted Comet performance by staging a 100-mph/100,000-mile durability run at the

As part of an effort to recapture its "hot-car" image of the 1950s, Mercury added a racier Comet during 1964. Aptly named Cyclone, this $2655 hardtop coupe packed a new 289 V-8 with a strong 210 horses. Also standard were firm suspension, chrome wheels, bucket seats, and floorshift.

1965

A full redesign for a banner Detroit year helped lift big-Merc sales to their highest level in eight seasons. The all-new '65s touted styling and engineering "In the Lincoln Continental tradition" to firmly link the two brands of Lincoln-Mercury Division. The Park Lane convertible (above) and Colony Park wagon (right) were the flagships.

Revised
for '65, Comet
styling was still a bit busy.
Calientes, shown below, retained
Buick-like front-fender "portholes."

1965

1966 COMET

Comet finally graduated from compact to a true midsize for 1966 by adopting the same underskin design as that year's new Ford Fairlane. Cyclone was now a top-line series with a hardtop coupe and convertible in regular and racier GT trim, the latter with bucket seats and bodyside stripes. A first-time 390 big-block V-8 option pumped GTs up to 335 horses.

The '66s were arguably the most-attractive Comets yet with their cleaner, curvier new lines. Prices spanned a broader lineup too, ranging from the $3152 Cyclone GT convertible (above, left to right), the $2790 Capri Villager station wagon, and the $2206 "202" two-door sedan.

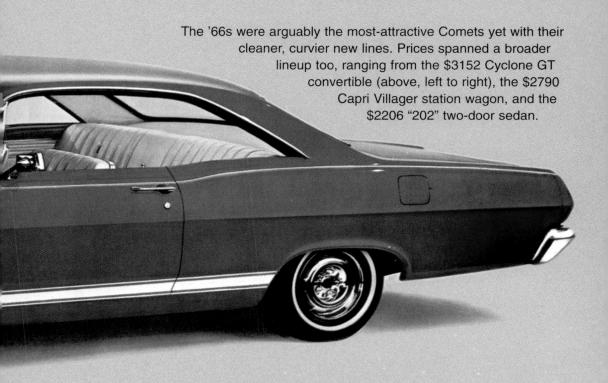

229

Mercury

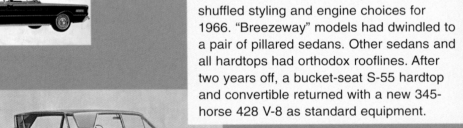

Still Fords beneath the skin, full-size Mercs shuffled styling and engine choices for 1966. "Breezeway" models had dwindled to a pair of pillared sedans. Other sedans and all hardtops had orthodox rooflines. After two years off, a bucket-seat S-55 hardtop and convertible returned with a new 345-horse 428 V-8 as standard equipment.

1967

Mercury's main 1967 news was the introduction of the Cougar, a longer, more luxurious version of the hot-selling Ford Mustang. It came only as a coupe with a 289 V-8 or, with the GT option, a big 390. This uplevel XR-7 model was done up as a show car honoring Mercury racing driver Dan Gurney (above).

Big Mercurys got slighty curvier lines for 1967, plus a centrally bulged hood and grille as a visual link to the latest Lincolns. Unpopular models were broomed, but Monterey and posh Park Lane convertibles continued. Monterey's ragtop (above) and hardtop offered a rarely ordered bucket-seat Sports Package that was sometimes seen with S-55 badges (below).

1968

Cougar didn't change its looks for 1968, nor the XR-7 model's posh interior with Jaguar-style dashboard (right). But available performance did change in a big way with addition of a potent GTE package and a limited-edition XR-7G (named for Dan Gurney) option. Both featured burly 428 V-8s with around 390 horses, plus other exclusive features.

Another round of styling and mechanical refinements marked 1968 full-size Mercurys like the posh Park Lane convertible. Optional wagon-style imitation wood bodyside trim arrived at midseason for the Park Lane convertible and hardtop coupe, but drew few orders and was promptly dropped. Mercury's major news for '68 was its redesigned midsize cars in an expanded lineup that included low-priced Comets, performance-focused Cyclones (above), and new comfort-oriented Montego models.

1969

Cougar added convertibles and more available power with a 1969 redesign. Big Mercurys were also clean-sheet fresh. A sporty Marauder "tunnelback" hardtop (right) joined the lineup. The Cyclone GT fastback (above right) returned with a potent new 335-horsepower 428 Cobra Jet V-8 option.

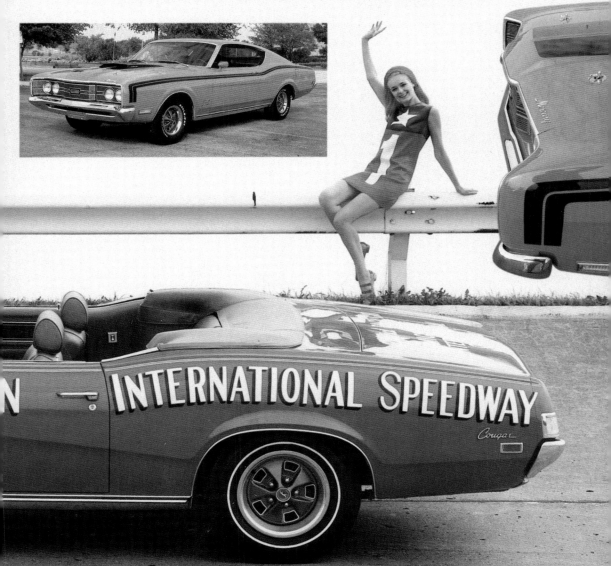

1960 OLDSMOBILE

Oldsmobile pried the tinsel off its all-new 1959s to create one of 1960's more-attractive cars. Offerings again spanned Dynamic 88s, Super 88s, and top-line Ninety-Eights. Each series included a convertible, a four-door hardtop, and two-door hardtops and sedans. The 88 lines also offered Fiesta wagons. Model-year sales dipped a bit, but Olds remained one of Detroit's healthier medium-price makes.

Every Olds was new for 1961, starting with F-85, the brand's first compact (far left). Standard models got thinner roof pillars, sculpted lower-body lines, and an equally expressive dashboard. A new Ninety-Eight Starfire convertible (lower left) featured standard bucket front seats.

1962

BLAZES NEW HEIGHTS IN SPINE-TINGLING PERFORMANCE!

Olds emphasized compact sportiness for 1962 with the bucket-seat Cutlass, offered in coupe and new convertible models. As before, an efficient 215 V-8 powered all F-85s. Full-size Oldsmobiles were restyled, but again relied on burly 394 V-8s. A new 345-horsepower version was featured in the Starfire convertible (far right).

1963 OLDSMOBILE

A crisp new look marked 1963 full-size Oldsmobiles. The buckets-and-console Starfire continued in convertible and hardtop coupe models. The Cutlass Jetfire returned from mid 1962 as a hardtop, plus the same new "big Olds" styling as other F-85s. Unique to Jetfire was an intriguing turbocharged V-8 with 215 horses, plus special trim. Only 5842 were built for '63, however.

Starfire

S-1963

JETFIRE

OLDSMOBILE

1963

OLDSMOBILE
FOR '64

WHERE THE ACTION IS!

Slightly more conservative styling was the 1964 direction for full-size Oldsmobiles (red cars pictured). The bucket-seat Starfire (below) breathed excitement into the line. Bigger news was transformation of the F-85 and Cutlass compacts (other cars pictured) into midsize cars. Still, Olds slipped from fifth to seventh in the production race for '64.

'65 OLDSMOBILE

Midsize Oldsmobiles for 1965 included novel Vista Cruiser wagons with a "split-level" skylight roof. Full-size models adopted curvier lines featuring "hop-up" rear fenders. Shown here are the flashy Starfire convertible and two-door hardtop.

442

Oldsmobile helped popularize the muscle car starting in 1964 with its Cutlass-based 4-4-2. Offered as a hardtop and convertible, the 4-4-2 returned for '65 packing a potent 400 V-8 with four-barrel carburetor and 345 horsepower. Also included were four-on-the-floor transmission, fat tires, uprated suspension and special trim. Though not the lightest or fastest of the breed, the 4-4-2 was plenty quick at around 7.5 seconds 0-60 mph. It was surprisingly agile too.

Olds enjoyed record sales for 1965 thanks largely to the popularity of its redesigned big cars. Among them were high-value Jetstar 88s (above), a sporty Jetstar I hardtop (right), and the posh top-of-the-line Ninety-Eights (below).

1966

For 1966, Olds designers forged a closer visual link between full-size models, like the Starfire (above) and midsize offerings, the rapid but refined 4-4-2 (below). Among the shared elements were squared-off front fenders, curvy rear fenderlines, and large bumpers. Model-year sales eased some, but again came close to a rousing 600,000.

Oldsmobile entered the prestigious personal-luxury market with the 1966 Toronado, the first American production car with front-wheel drive since the late 1930s. Handsome as well as innovative, the Toronado was unmistakable with its muscular wheel bulges, sleek fastback roofline, neatly cropped tail, and flip-up headlights. Today, it's a modern classic.

For such a large luxury car, the Toronado was a real stormer. [It de]bowed with a 425 V-8 making 385 horses and a massive 47[5] pound-feet of torque. The only transmission was an automat[ic,] a special version of General Motors' smooth Turbo-Hydrama[tic.]

1967

1967

1967

Optional front-disc brakes were among the few changes for the 1967 Toronado (left). Ads now courted women buyers (right), but sales plunged. Oldsmobile's mid-size cars were more popular than ever for '67 despite only evolutionary changes. Below: a low-frills 4-4-2 hardtop.

Next to mink, Toronado is the most exciting animal around.

(Who says it's a man's world?)

The nicest thing outside of a mink is the inside of a Toronado. Mark how Toronado doors open wide to let you glide in and out easily, even in the frilliest of frocks. Flat floors, front and rear, let you sit in the center like a lady. Now take the wheel. Toronado's front wheel drive negotiates tight turns, deep snow and rugged terrain effortlessly. And makes pulling into a parking place as easy as pulling on a kid glove. Would you say Toronado is a man's kind of car? Indeed. The kind of a car a man buys for his kind of girl!

There's a Rocket for every pocket at your Olds Dealer's One-Stop Transportation Center: 36 Toronado-inspired Oldsmobile models—with a wider range of prices, colors and standard safety equipment than ever.

Engineered for excitement...Toronado-style!

OLDSMOBILE | GM

Oldsmobile for '68

New at Olds for 1968 were a facelifted Toronado (above, left) and redesigned midsize models with swoopy lines and many new features. Leadfoots again flocked to the 4-4-2s (below and right).

Toronado influence was evident in big-Olds styling for '68, as on the popular Delta 88 hardtop sedan (above) and posh Ninety-Eight convertible (below). The Cutlass wagon also looked good in its new '68 duds.

Escape from the ordinary

STARRING THE 1969 OLDSMOBILES

442

Olds advertising took a slightly humorous turn by 1969, when big cars sprouted pointy fronts. A huge 455 V-8 returned for an updated Toronado (left) and as a new option for the hot 4-4-2s. Meantime, Oldsmobile's mainstream midsizers—like the Cutlass wagon pictured below—were fast becoming one of America's top-selling car lines.

PLYMOUTH
1960

Plymouth began the 1960s with a full design featuring welded "Unibody" construction and new styling with some of Detroit's biggest tailfins. George Jetson would have loved it. The top engine option (top) was a new "Golden Commando" 383 V-8 with 330 brawny horses.

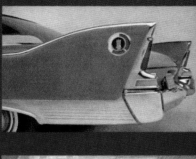

Though not labeled as a Plymouth, the new 1960 Valiant compact (above) was a sales boost for Chrysler Corporation's bread-and-butter brand. The 1960 full-size Plymouths were hard to miss with their giant new fins. Still available for those models was a novel "Highway Hi-Fi" record player (left).

Valiant formally became part of the Plymouth line for 1961 and added two-door models including a snappy hardtop (below). All Valiants furnished the most pep and best handling among the Big Three compacts, but were again way outsold by Ford's rival Falcon.

Big Plymouths were dramatically restyled for 1961 with a rather dubious front end and finless rear fenders. The dashboard would have been at home in an alien spaceship.

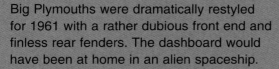

1962

Valiant
answered
the fast-growing
consumer clamor for
sportier compacts with
the 1962 Signet 200 hardtop coupe
(top). Featured were special styling touches and an
all-vinyl interior with front bucket seats and floorshift.
Plymouth priced it at just $2230, but sales were modest.

In another dramatic shift, Plymouth "downsized" its larger models for 1962 and applied Valiant-like styling. The cars were lighter, and thus quicker, thriftier, and more agile, but they were a tough sell against traditional-size Fords and Chevrolets.

1963

PLYMOUTH

SUPER STOCK

426

"Big" Plymouths looked more orthodox for 1963, but sold little better than the '62s. Still, a brutish new 426 "wedgehead" V-8 option with 370-425 horses made these cars some of the fastest around. Its main mission was to make Plymouth a power in Super Stock drag racing. It did.

A 1963 redesign (above) started Valiant on a long run as one of America's most perennially popular cars. The new models included convertibles for the first time, but all still offered peppy and durable "Slant Six" engines in two sizes.

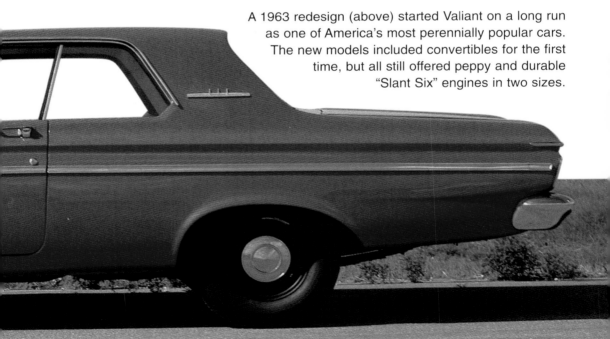

1964

The Valiant-based Barracuda "glassback" bowed during 1964 as a sportier Plymouth compact. Its main rival was Ford's hot-selling new Mustang.

Big-Plymouth sales were recovering by 1964, helped by another restyle of the basic '62 design. Back for a third season as the top-line offerings were the Sport Fury hardtop and convertible with standard front bucket seats and shift console–hood ornaments announced the buyer's choice of V-8 power, which included 361-, 383-, and big 426-cubic-inch options.

1965

Plymouth's lineup of "Roaring '65s" reinstated true full-size models, all called Fury and led by bucket-seat Sport Furys (right). Barracuda (above) saw few changes for '65, but again shared a lively 273-cube V-8 option with Valiants.

The ill-starred 1962 Plymouth design got new styling and a new lease on life as the "midsize" 1965 Belvedere (above). A broad lineup included wagons and sporty bucket-seat Satellite models.

Let yourself Go Plymouth '66

Plymouth's big news for 1966 involved all-new midsize cars (left). Available was a new street version of the 426 Hemi V-8 from NASCAR racing.

Valiant (far left) and Barracuda got squared-up front ends as one of their main changes for 1966. All could be quite quick when optioned with the lively 235-horse 273 V-8.

Big Plymouths weren't much changed for '66, but moved with the times by adding luxury-trimmed VIP models (right) above the Sport Furys (below).

Plymouth is out to win you over.

'67

Plymouth supported its 1967 ad slogan with many new models. A redesigned Barracuda fastback gained hardtop (right) and convertible siblings. Belvedere added GTX "muscle" models (below) with a standard 440-cube V-8.

Plymouth pulled out two more stops in its quest for 1967 sales with complete redesigns for the big Fury (above) and compact Valiant (below). They rounded out a very strong lineup, yet Plymouth couldn't budge from fourth place in overall industry sales. One reason was still-stronger competition from Ford and Chevy.

1968

Barracuda went in for trendy 1968 "flower power" with a new trim option for the hardtop (right). It was groovy, but not that popular. This year's big Furys received deft cosmetic updates. A more-rakish "Fast Top" roofline was new for certain hardtop coupes, including the Sport Fury version (below).

Plymouth scored a hit with the 1968 Road Runner, a "budget" muscle car with a strong 335-horse 383 V-8, tight suspension and no-nonsense styling. The tie-in with the beloved Warner Bros. cartoon character was marketing genius. Young hotbloods loved the car's beep-beep horn and bird decals.

1969

Plymouth used "mod" artwork to push midsize muscle for 1969. And properly equipped, the Road Runner and GTX were as fearsome as these images suggest.

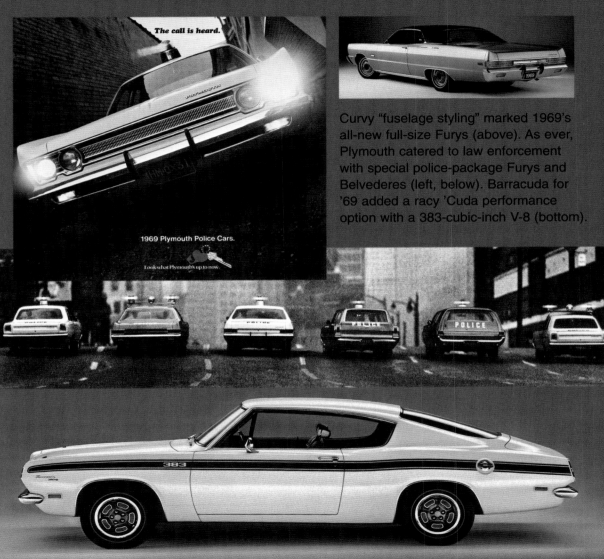

The call is heard.

PLYMOUTH

1969 Plymouth Police Cars.

Look what Plymouth's up to now.

Curvy "fuselage styling" marked 1969's all-new full-size Furys (above). As ever, Plymouth catered to law enforcement with special police-package Furys and Belvederes (left, below). Barracuda for '69 added a racy 'Cuda performance option with a 383-cubic-inch V-8 (bottom).

383

POLICE

POLICE

PONTIAC
1960

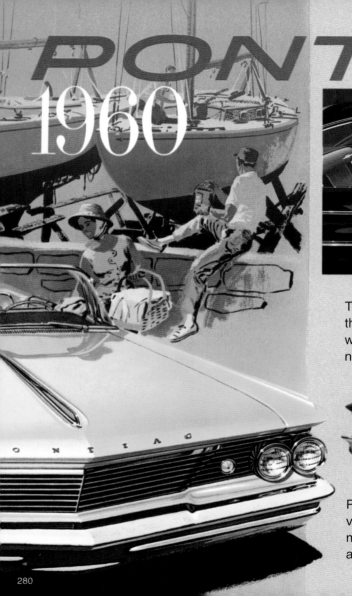

The 1960 Pontiacs sold even better than the all-new '59s on which they were based. Fresh styling and new colors aided the cause.

Pontiac again promoted the handling virtues of its "Wide Track" design, a marketing gem that also enhanced the appearance of its cars.

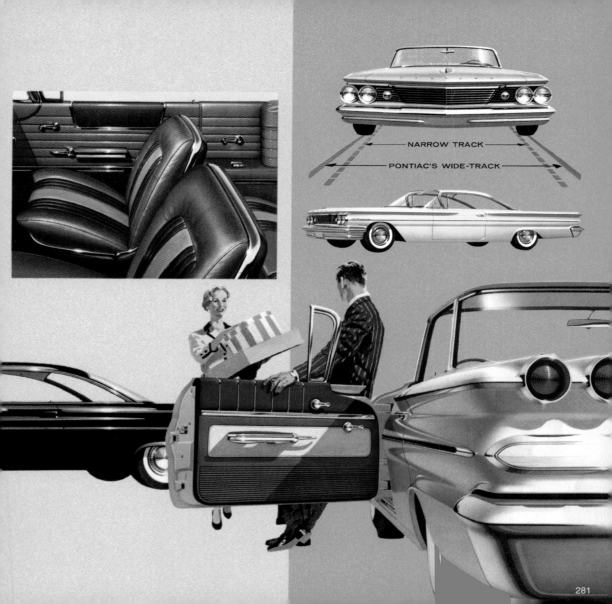

NARROW TRACK

PONTIAC'S WIDE-TRACK

1961

Crisp new styling and a little less weight marked the redesigned 1961 Pontiacs. Models still ran the gamut from an affordable Catalina two-door sedan to the luxurious, fun-loving Bonneville convertible (below).

Pontiac joined Detroit's swing to compacts with the 1961 Tempest (right). It offered coupes, sedans, and wagons with a standard four-cylinder engine, optional V-8, and novel rear-mount transmissions.

Wide-Track PONTIAC '62

Big Pontiacs got fresh looks for 1962. Also new was Grand Prix, a sport-luxury hardtop with snazzy bucket-seat interior. The GP was an instant hit, and over 30,000 were sold.

LE MANS

Tempests also got a styling update for 1962. Convertibles and sport coupes again offered a LeMans trim option with front bucket seats and other sporty-car features that buyers now wanted in compacts.

Pontiac was a Detroit styling leader by 1963, when it unveiled new-look full-size models led by top-line Bonnevilles (above). The even prettier Grand Prix (right) has become a collector's item.

A lower-body restyle made 1963 Tempests look more like big Pontiacs (top). They could also perform more like full-size models, with the new optional 260-horsepower 326-cubic-inch V-8. A 225-horse four was standard.

1964

Big Pontiacs looked a bit huskier and "softer" for 1964. Ads and brochures still relied largely on stylish illustrations that posed the cars in pretty settings and made them seem even more attractive.

Pontiac invented the "muscle car" with the GTO option for its redesigned 1964 Tempest (right). Starting around $3000, the GTO delivered a four-barrel 389 V-8 with 325 horses, plus firm suspension and unique cosmetic touches. Demand instantly outpaced Pontiac's projections, and a performance legend was born.

'65

Big Pontiacs added inches and pounds for 1965, but nicely hid their bulk with flowing new body lines. Slanted Grand Prix-style rooflines were now featured on all two-door hardtops, including the Catalina 2+2 version (left) with bucket seats, floor shift, and a standard 338-horse 421 V-8.

The midsize 1966 Tempests and LeMans sported stacked headlamps *à la* full-size Pontiacs. GTOs offered up to 360 red-hot horses.

1966

Choice was the key to automotive success in the 1960s, and Pontiac was no exception. For 1966, its big-car line alone offered 17 models, including the flagship Grand Prix (bottom), plus trim options like a Ventura package (below) with extra brightwork and upgraded interior. A vinyl roof covering and whitewall tires were among the many other extras offered to tempt new-car shoppers.

Reflecting its strong popularity, the GTO graduated from an option package to a model series for 1966. All midsize Pontiacs were redesigned with clean, curvy new styling and somewhat larger dimensions, but only GTO was advertised as "The Tiger."

1967

Pontiac was surprisingly bold in offering a European-style overhead-cam six-cylinder engine for Tempests, plus a higher-output Sprint option identified by special badges and body striping (above and left). But Pontiac's big news that year was the introduction of the Firebird "ponycar." (below). Though based on Chevrolet's new '67 Camaro, Firebird had Pontiac engines and styling cues, plus slightly more-upscale trim and pricing.

Pontiac marked its sixth year as Detroit's third best-seller in 1967. This was the only model year the glamorus Grand Prix was available in a convertible body style (left).

Pontiac's midsize models were little-changed for '67. The GTO remained the image leader and accounted for 82,000 of the 782,734 cars the division built that year. All GTOs had a 389-cubic-inch V-8.

Still the division other carmakers eyed for youthful styling, Pontiac again altered the appearance of its full-size models, including the racy 2+2 ragtop (right).

1968

Firebird wasn't greatly changed for 1968 (above), but other Pontiacs picked up its protruding "beak" as a new brand signature. Midsize models were redesigned, led by hot GTOs with noses wrapped in body-color plastic for an ultraclean look.

GTO

1968

'69

Pontiac scored another hit with its redesigned 1969 Grand Prix (foreground). Now more midsize than full-size car, it offered elegant styling with the industry's longest hood, plus a standard 350-horse 400 V-8. Pontiac sold a smashing 112,000-plus.

The '69
Pontiac line
also featured restyled
Firebirds (above) and the
always–fab GTO (top).

RAMBLER

1960

Surfing a wave of compact-car popularity American Motors sold some 450,000 of its 1960 Ramblers, the highest tally ever for an independent U.S. automaker. The lineup included Rebels (above) and larger, upscale Ambassadors (left).

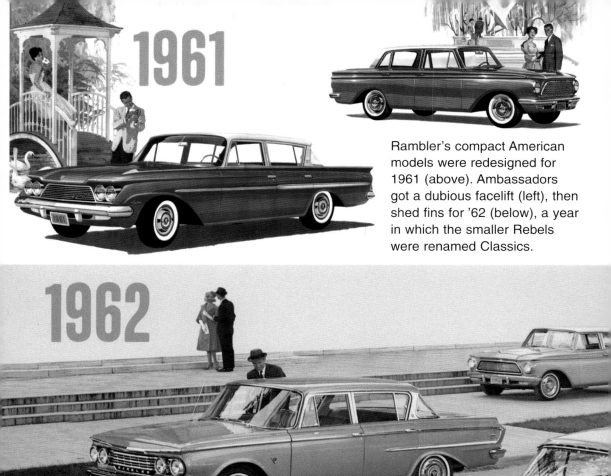

1961

Rambler's compact American models were redesigned for 1961 (above). Ambassadors got a dubious facelift (left), then shed fins for '62 (below), a year in which the smaller Rebels were renamed Classics.

1962

1963

For 1963,
the Rambler Classics and
Ambassadors were fully redesigned
for the first time since the mid 1950s. Both shared
trimmer new bodies with curved side glass and innovative
"Uniside" door frames, plus AMC's established unit-
body/frame construction. The American compacts
kept their older, boxy unitized design (as on
the red convertible). AMC
fell to fifth in the
industry sales
race.

Rambler Classic added hardtop coupes for 1964 (right). So did the Ambassador line. The American was redesigned as a cut-down Classic with similarly clean, simple styling (above right). AMC wagons remained quite popular.

1965

AMC billed its 1965 models as "The Sensible Spectaculars." A lower-body restyle added length and visual pizzazz to Classics (above) and Ambassadors. Also new was the Classic-based Marlin (below), a five-passenger Mustang fighter with sporty interior and "fastback" roof. It wasn't very popular.

1966

The 1966 AMC Ambassador was the 1965 Rambler model with a few updates, including a posh new DPL 2-door hardtop (below). Rambler Classics (left) and Americans (above) again offered nice blends of sportiness and economy.

1967

AMC styling went from mundane to mod with the curvy, somewhat larger Rambler Rebel that replaced the Classic for 1967 (right). That year's Ambassador shared the new look and was now the basis for the Marlin fastback (below), which drew just 4547 sales in a mixed year for AMC.

1968

The Rambler American Rogue returned for 1968 with an available V-8 that made it quite snappy. Even more exciting were the sporty new Javelin ponycar (left) and a unique two-seat offshoot called AMX (below). Javelin sold well for an AMC product, drawing over 56,000 orders.

1969

The Rambler American took its final bow for 1969 (below). Among the few additions were a wild-looking performance hardtop, the SC/Rambler (aka Scrambler), with a 315-horse 390 V-8. Just 1512 were built. A more-imposing new front end marked that year's big AMC Ambassadors (below).

Studebaker

Studebaker traced its carmaking heritage to 1902, and peaked in the 1940s. By 1960, it was a bit player with just two cars lines, the Hawk (above) and the more-popular Lark family of 6- and 8-cylinder compacts.

1961

Lark sales plunged nearly 50 percent for 1961, despite a heavy restyle with a hint of European design. Quad headlamps were a new feature for uplevel Regal models. Lark's jaunty hardtop coupe (below) added an optional "Skytop" vinyl sunroof that pushed back by hand for open-air fun.

1962

Studebaker posted a small sales gain for 1962. Lark helped with freshened looks and a sporty new bucket-seat Daytona hardtop and convertible. Adding needed glamour to the line was the Gran Turismo Hawk (above), an artful makeover of Studey's familiar "family sports car." It drew a respectable 8388 sales.

1963

Intended to bolster Studebaker's sagging image, the new-for-'63 Avanti sports coupe (below) was a design triumph but a commercial flop. That year's GT Hawk (above) got only detail changes, as did most Larks (right).

1964

Studebaker closed its historic South Bend, Indiana, plant in 1964 amid fast-falling sales. The GT Hawk was again little-changed. So was the singular Avanti (left). Larks got an effective restyle, but buyers now doubted Studebaker's future and mostly stayed away.

1965

Studebaker fought to survive in '65 with a smaller set of Lark-based sedans and wagons. They were much like the '64s, but were built in Canada with Chevrolet engines instead of the old Studebaker units. Avanti and Hawk were dropped.

The 1965 Studebakers showed few outward changes. A sporty two-door Daytona and posh Cruiser sedan (right) continued.

1966

Studebaker managed a mild facelift for 1966, but only 8947 sales. With that, the firm closed shop and moved into other types of business.

The final Studebakers got a simple face unique to the '66 models, plus functional air-extractor vents added above the taillamps. Time had run out for Studebaker, which lacked funds and facilities to develop new models—and enjoyed little public confidence in its name.

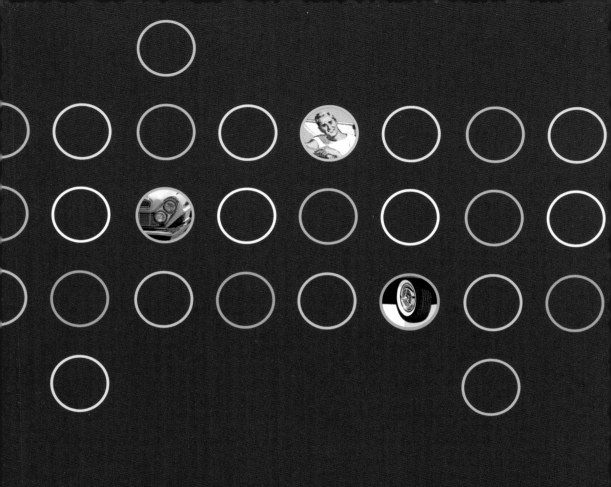

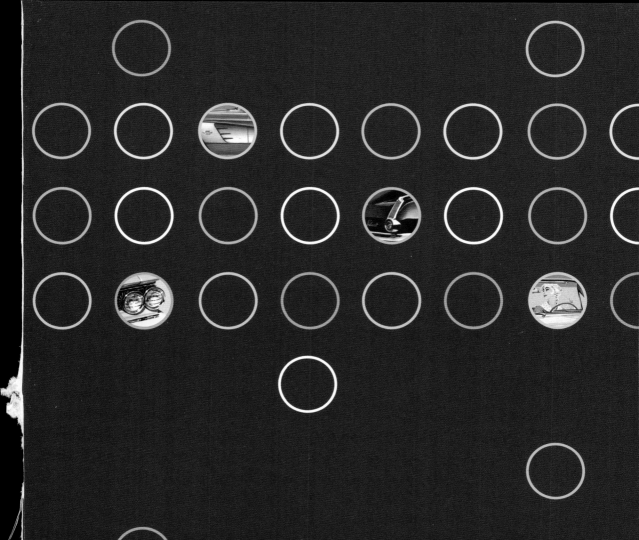

Production Numbers
FOR THE 1960s

Chevrolet • 20,333,083
Ford • 17,067,193
Pontiac • 6,761,759
Plymouth • 6,301,993
Oldsmobile • 4,980,463
Buick • 4,932,153
Dodge • 4,652,198
Rambler • 3,615,165

Mercury • 3,333,790
Cadillac • 1,802,826
Chrysler • 1,800,221
Studebaker • 404,130
Lincoln • 397,459
Imperial • 168,971
DeSoto • 29,115
Edsel • 3,008